# Remembering Ola Rotimi:

## A Complete Man of the Theatre

# Remembering Ola Rotimi:

## A Complete Man of the Theatre

**Essays & Tributes**

Edited by

**Bisi Adigun**

ISBN: 978-978-794-258-1



Editor: Bisi Adigun

Cover Design: Kunle Ajose

Published in Nigeria by:
**Bowen University Press**
Iwo, Osun State, Nigeria

Phone: +2348123054266
Email Address: Olabisi.adigun@bowen.edu.ng
Website: https://bowen.edu.ng

# CONTENTS

# DEDICATION

Oba Segun Akinbola
Biyi Bandele
Uko Atai

And many, many others who have wrapped themselves up with earth like duvet

# ACKNOWLEDGEMENTS

*Eni ba mo inu ro, o di dandan ki o mo ope du.* Bearing in mind this Yoruba witticism, which I shall loosely translate here as, S/he who knows how to think must surely know how to thank, I think it is extremely important to thank a number of people who contributed directly or indirectly to the success of the webinar on Ola Rotimi in 2020 and/or the tedious process of turning the idea of a book arising from the proceedings at the webinar into this reality.

First, I would like to thank all those who were at the script conference back in July 2020 where I came up with the idea of remembering Ola Rotimi on the 20th anniversary of his death. Leke Akinrowo, Wole Adeniyi, Bimbo Manuel, Francis Nwoche, Makinde Adeniran, Elsie Uvie Oluku, Kate Adepegba, Omowunmi Dada, I thank you.

Prof Grace Olutayo, thanks a lot for agreeing with me that the idea of remembering Ola Rotimi was a great one when I first mooted it. You did not only enable the webinar, you ensured it was a resounding success. If you had thought or acted otherwise, there would not have been a webinar that has culminated in this book. You are indeed a grace to College of Liberal Studies, Bowen University and the whole humanity at large. And I pray that may your grace continue to be with us.

I must also express my profound gratitude to Dr Stanley Ohenhen, the amiable Programme Coordinator of the Theatre Arts Programme, because by the time the idea of the webinar got to his table, it had already gone to the Acting Provost and the VC. However, it did not bother him; he rallied around the idea and contributed in no small way to the success of the webinar.

All the resource persons who participated in the webinar to make it a success, including Prof Emanuel Emesealu, Mr Tunji Ojeyemi, and Prof Femi Osofisan; to those who participated and have contributed to this volume to make it a reality, I appreciate each and everyone of you. Profs Akanji Nasiru, Olu Obafemi, Duro Oni, Julie Umukoro, Dr Emmanuel Nwachuku, Mr Bimbo Manuel, Mr Enitan Rotimi, and Mr Austin Awulonu (though did not present at the webinar), thanks.

I must also express my deep gratitude to Honourable Daramola for organising the press conference through which the awareness for the webinar was created. Also, I would like to express my thanks to the personnel of the Bowen University's Directorate of Digital Services (DDS), namely Fiyinfoluwa Adewale,

Kayode Adebayo, and Yomi Odewenwa for doing Bowen University proud on the day of the webinar with your sense of dedication and professionalism.

I would like to also thank Prof Duro Oni for his excellent idea that motivated me to contact Prof Wole Soyinka; he was also there for me to offer advice on how to order the presentation as well as how much time to allocate to each speaker. And, I must not forget my ever-busy but always helpful brother Oooga Jahman Anikulapo for advising me on the best way to enthuse WS with the idea of contributing to the webinar.

My thanks also go to all our peer reviewers Dr Owen Sanders (Tshwane University of Technology, RSA), Prof Niyi Coker (San Diego University), Dr Asselin Charles retired Professor of Comparative Literature, Dr Kolawole Adeniyi (Obafemi Awolowo University, Ile-Ife), and, last but not least, Dr James Gibbs (teacher and critic) who doubled up as a supervising editor for this project. Thanks to you all for making this publication a much better one.

I also must thank: the Chief Librarian of Bowen University, Iwo, Mrs Grace Otunla for all her support and assistance when we were deliberating on how best to get the ISBN for this book; Mr Ayo Umoh of Surewords Publication, who as our consultant, assisted us in a lot of ways at the beginning of this project; Mr Kunle Ajose for the design of the e-flier for the webinar in 2020 and for the cover of this book; and, last but not least, the hardworking, amiable, ever-helpful Kolade Olanrewaju Freedom of DeftTouch Publishers. Truth be told, without Kolade's expertise and professionalism, this book would not have come out like this. Kolade simply knows how things ought to be done and when they ought to be done; that is why this book has come out as it ought to. Thanks for all your hard work and sleepless nights, Kolade.

I must also say a big thank you to Prof Joshua Ogunwole (aka The Coach) for giving me back my mojo when I lost it due to the antics of a senior colleague who was meant to co-edit this book with me. May the good lord continue to bless you real good, Coach.

Lastly, I want to thank my Creator, who is the Alpha and Omega, for making it possible for the webinar to be a success. It was the webinar that has birthed the idea of a book on Ola Rotimi which has now become a reality. *Ade ori okin, ki se fun eye keye. Anu ni a ri gba.* (The crown on the Ostrich head is not for all kinds of birds). In other words, it is by His special grace that this book has come to be.

Bisi Adigun (PhD)
*Iwo Osun State, October 2022*

# FOREWORD

Hello, everyone. You are welcome to this webinar. This webinar is in the honour of the passing of a renowned playwright, Emanuel Gladstone Rotimi, popularly known as Ola Rotimi that died 18th August, 2000. It is a good thing to remember the works of great minds that have come our way in life. Even though I am a soil scientist, I grew up to hear the name called and it keeps resonating all through my life. Ola Rotimi, Ola Rotimi, Ola Rotimi.

Ola Rotimi was a prolific and skilful playwright whose works reflect the diversity that Nigeria stands for. Ola Rotimi was a man of excellence; Ola Rotimi was a man that I would say epitomizes or epitomized accountability; Ola Rotimi had a great sense of responsibility; and, of course, Ola Rotimi had a drive for hard work. These are things that Bowen University stands for. So, the man, Ola Rotimi fits into our mode: Excellence and Godliness. Since it takes champions to eulogise the works of other champions, I want to congratulate the Theatre Arts Programme for planning and putting this webinar together.

Bowen University is indeed proud to host great minds like you, today. Our desire would have been that physically we can gather; physically we can celebrate, we can dance, we can beat drums and we can dress in diverse regalia to celebrate this man. But Covid 19 would not allow us to do these. So, we are going to be celebrating him this way, trusting that in the years ahead, Covid 19 would have gone, and we will be able to gather together as a small community in Bowen to really celebrate the man as would have loved to do.

We are indeed proud to celebrate two decades of the exit of this icon, Ola Rotimi. I wish you an enriching and inspiring deliberation. I hope and believe that as we discuss the works of this man, the ideals of this man – even from the great beyond – his life will speak to many of us, and spur many of us to move and do great things even in our life and career.

So, with this, I welcome you and declare this webinar open in the name of God the Father, the Son and the Holy Spirit.

Thank you and God bless.

Prof Joshua Ogunwole (The Coach)
*Vice Chancellor, Bowen University, Iwo*

## A Few Wise Words from Himself

The essence of this paper is a call to Third World theatre scholars and practitioners to pause and ponder on our past, so as to enable us to confront the present and future on a more informed footing. For a culture long harried by the buffetings of colonial subjugation, the call to pause and ponder seems appropriate, particularly in the present techno-economic lapse into a 'consumer' sub-world. For our young generation of theatre arts students and practitioners, a generation giddy with the 'identity crisis' arising from Euro-American cultural radiations, the call to pause and ponder over what we watch, and what we read and what we are told, seems compelling. Only through pausing and pondering on our past, can we, with a measure of self-confidence, engage in a discussion relating to the foreign and the familiar, on the probabilities of cultural syncretism rather than on the affirmations of cultural imperialism. Only then would, for instance the relationship between our familiar theatre and the foreign be akin to what the folklore of our forbears tell us about the basis of equality between the vulture and the ape. Day after day, the vulture flaunted his baldness at the ape. The ape got tired one evening and said to vulture:

> "Say, mister cut out the display!
> After all when we boil it down,
> What do you have that I don't?
> You're bald in the head?
> Well I am bald in the bottom.
> So there..." (Rotimi 1990, 60)*

---

* Rotimi, Ola. 1990. 'Much Ado about Brecht' in Fischer-Lichte, Erika, Josephine Riley and Michael Gissenwehrer (eds.). *The Dramatic Touch of Difference: Theatre Own and Foreign*. Gunter Narr Verlag Tubingen. 253-261.

# INTRODUCTION

## Ola Rotimi: Gone Forever, But Never Forgotten

*Bisi Adigun*

This book, without any shadow of doubt, is one of the most important significant outcomes of the webinar that was organised by the Theatre Arts Programme of Bowen University, Iwo on 18th August 2020 to commemorate the 20th anniversary of the death of Prof Olawale Gladstone Rotimi. However, it must be made clear that but for the timely and serendipitous intervention of Prof Joshua Ogunwole, the indefatigable Vice Chancellor of Bowen University, on 17th August, 2022, the idea of this publication would have remained a figment of my imagination. How do I mean?

The idea to organise an event to commemorate the 20th anniversary of Ola Rotimi's death struck me sometime in June 2020. Covid 19 had already, at the time, wreaked havoc around the world, but the restrictions that accompanied the pandemic were gradually being relaxed. So, I attended, in the company of some colleagues who are working in the entertainment industry, a script conference that was held at Afinju Concept International (ACI) multimedia studios in Lekki, Lagos. It was for a film script that a friend, Leke Akinrowo, wanted to write for True Life Productions. After the exciting and stimulating script conference that lasted about six hours, we began to talk about the state of Nigerian theatre. Our discussion soon dovetailed into how things had changed since our undergraduate days; it was in that context that Rotimi's name came up.

I was living in Ireland in 2000 when Rotimi died suddenly a few months after the passing of his beloved wife, Hazel, so I did not feel the impact of his untimely death as I would have were I in Nigeria at the time. It was perhaps for the same reason that it did not occur to me that it was that long ago that he died. When it finally dawned on me through further discussion with my friends that come August 2020 it was going to be exactly 20 years that Rotimi passed on, I felt really disappointed and saddened that such a great man of theatre died suddenly almost twenty years ago and no one seemed to be planning anything to commemorate the anniversary. It was there and then that I promised myself that some kind of event must be put together to honour one of the most gifted theatre makers that Nigeria and indeed Africa has ever produced.

Upon returning to Bowen University in Iwo, I discussed the idea with Dr (now Prof) Grace Olutayo, who was then the Acting Provost of the College of Liberal Studies, where the Theatre Arts Programme is domiciled. She agreed that it was a good idea, so she asked me to put a proposal together, which she in turn submitted directly to the Vice Chancellor. Although, a soil scientist, as he himself has indicated in the Foreword to this book, our VC, who we also fondly call The Coach, is a dilettante right from his university days at Ahmadu Bello University (ABU), Zaria. So, he is always very supportive of all our activities in the Theatre Arts Programme. Furthermore, he personally considers Ola Rotimi a national icon whom he holds in high regard. It is no surprise therefore that he gave the idea of a webinar to remember Ola Rotimi 20 years after his death all the support that it required.

Thus, on 18th August 2020, at 10 am Nigerian time, the webinar, which was themed 'Remembering Ola Rotimi, A Complete Man of the Theatre: 20 Years On', was declared open by the Coach, after which Oba Segun Akinbola, who was the royal father of the day, gave his opening address. Then, Profs Akanji Nasiru, Olu Obafemi, and Duro Oni gave their presentations for ten minutes each. It was then the turn of Mr Bimbo Manuel, our first discussant, to talk about Ola Rotimi as a teacher. After Manuel, who, as a matter of fact, was the facilitator of the script conference that I mentioned earlier, Prof Julie Umukoro presented her talk. Then, Prof Emanuel Emesealu and Dr Emmanuel Nwachuku, our first discussant, followed suit.

Unfortunately, Mr Peter Badejo who was our second discussant had trouble logging in on the day and was unable to make his presentation. However, he has since revised his presentation for inclusion in this volume for the benefit of those who would like to know what it was like working closely with Ola Rotimi for many years. I also had the privilege to conduct a recorded interview with Wole Soyinka a few days before the webinar. The interview was played after Dr Nwachuku's presentation as Soyinka's contribution to the webinar. To bring the webinar to a close, Enitan Rotimi, Ola Rotimi's first born gave us a rare glimpse into the world of Ola Rotimi as a father not only to his biological children, but also to all those he held very dear.

The webinar was not only a session of holding talks, however (if you would pardon the pun), Mr Tunji Ojeyemi, who, like Badejo, had had the opportunity to work closely with Rotimi for decades, started us off with a solo performance of extracts from Ola Rotimi's historical tragedy, *Kurunmi*. Similarly, the students of the Theatre Arts Programme presented a zoom performance of an extract from Rotimi's play, *Man Talk, Woman Talk* about an hour into the webinar. To round up the webinar, a video recording of the Yoruba version of Ola Rotimi's historical tragedy, *Kurunmi,* which was produced by Leke Akinrowo of Riveting Integrated Entertainment and directed by Muyiwa Oshinaike, was played. That was how the remembering of the life of Ola Rotimi came to its glorious end.

Born on April 13, 1938, Rotimi was unarguably one of the most celebrated Nigerian playwrights cum theatre directors. Aside from being an ingenious playwright of historical plays, which usually reflect Nigeria's cultural diversity, Ola Rotimi was an occasional actor, choreographer, designer, he was also the founder of the Ori Olokun Theatre in the late 1960s. When he returned to Ife from Port Harcourt in 1991, Rotimi founded the African Cradle Theatre (ACT) with which he mounted a number of spectacular productions of his plays with financial support from Nigerian Industrial Bank (NIB). I had the privilege in 1992 of watching late Ayo Akinwale in the lead role of the NIB-sponsored production of *Ovonramwen Nogbaisi* at the main hall of the University of Lagos. I recall that I was so viscerally affected by the way the Oba of Benin is treated in the play that I vowed never to wear tie to work again thenceforth. According to Ojetunji Ojeyemi, who was the Production Manager of African Cradle Theatre, there were two other productions subsequently that were also sponsored by NIB. *Hopes of the Living Dead,* as directed by Ola Rotimi, was on a national tour in 1993, followed by the production in 1995 of *Kurunmi* at the Law School auditorium in Victoria Island, Lagos.

Ola Rotimi, standing in the extreme left in the front row, with company members of the African Cradle Theatre (ACT), circa 1992. (Photo, courtesy of Ojetunji Ojeyemi)

Ola Rotimi's humility and love for the people is palpable from the above picture. Indeed, "great minds don't hug the limelight", as the Coach has put it to me in one of our WhatsApp chats, "rather limelight seeks out such minds to hug".

I should perhaps seize this opportunity to set the record straight here that the dream project Rotimi was working on before his sudden death in Ile-Ife at the age of 62, according to Ojeyemi in my telephone interview with him on 15 September 2022, was the revival of the Ori Olokun Theatre for Obafemi Awolowo University with a stage performance that would have involved a strong cast of 1000 performers, contrary to the hitherto purported number that had been put between 3000 and 5000 (see, for instance, Duro Oni's chapter in this volume and Maria Diamond in *The Guardian* edition of 15 August, 2020). Regardless of the actual number of cast that Rotimi would have deployed, however, the cold hands of death had robbed us of his most ambitious project. But his legacy will continue to live on in the plays he left behind, particularly, his popular plays.

His most staged plays that made him the darling of total theatre lovers at home and abroad, include *The Gods Are Not to Blame* (1968), *Kurunmi* (1969) and *Ovonramwen Nogbaisi* (1971). Rotimi was also the author of *Our Husband Has Gone Mad* (1966), *Holding Talks* (1970), *Grip Am* (1973), *If: A Tragedy of the Ruled* (1979), and *Hopes of the Living Dead* (1985). While his well-known plays are highly spectacular and entertaining, his philosophical position in all of his plays can be distilled into three levels: (i) to promote inter-ethnic solidarity; [ii] to domesticate the English language with a view to making it accessible to all and sundry; and [iii] to highlight the advantages of good leadership in our society. Rotimi's most significant contribution to the development of Nigerian theatre, however, was the way in which he deployed theatre to foster a linkage between the town and the gown. In other words, his *raison d'être,* upon returning to Nigeria in 1966 as a Boston University directing graduate and the proud holder of an MFA in playwriting from Yale, was to create an active theatre that will appeal to and resonate not only with university dons on campus, but also the entire populace of the community of Ile Ife town.

It is no surprise therefore that Rotimi, though western-trained, ended up creating his own unique and accessible populist Nigerian theatre, highly influenced by traditional theatre forms and indigenous performance space, which was geared towards bridging the gap between the so-called popular theatre tradition (exemplified by the likes of Hubert Ogunde and Kola Ogunmola, on the one hand), and the literary theatre tradition (epitomized by the works of first generation Nigerian playwrights such as Wole Soyinka and J. P Clark, on the other hand), which is the main focus of Akanji Nasiru in this volume. It was against this background that Rotimi co-founded the Ori Olokun Centre as soon as he arrived in and started working as a research fellow in the mid-1960s with the Institute of African Studies at the then University of Ife (now Obafemi Awolowo University). He situated the Theatre Centre in Arubidi, a hinterland of the ancient city of Ile Ife, rather than on the university campus (see Peter Badejo's contribution in chapter five and my interview in chapter nine in this volume for more on this), and by so doing, Rotimi brought the gown and town together by grooming a group of talented performers and at the same time developing an audience base both on and off campus for his theatrical productions that never failed to enthrall.

Aside from being a complete man of the theatre, however, Rotimi also lectured at the then University of Ife from 1969 until he took an appointment at the University of Port Harcourt in 1977. Although he returned briefly to Ife in 1990, due to the harsh political conditions in Nigeria in the 1990s, he left Nigeria for the Caribbean and later proceeded to the US, where he taught at the Macalester College in St Paul, Minnesota in America. He eventually returned to Ile-Ife where he passed away in 2000. So Rotimi was an erudite scholar and one of the greatest practitioners of theatre that Nigeria has ever produced. He is an irreplaceable loss to the Nigerian theatre and global theatre at large and therefore sorely missed. It is thus with the famous line in the Nigerian national anthem, "The labour of our heroes past shall never be in vain", in mind that the webinar was orgnanised and hosted by Bowen University in 2020 to ensure that, though gone, our Ola Rotimi, a complete man of the theatre, is never forgotten.

While the webinar has since been edited and uploaded unto YouTube for posterity, as promised in the proposal that was submitted to the VC, I completely lost interest in the laudable idea of publishing this book when I began to be confronted by seemingly insurmountable obstacles. Until the VC called me out of the blue on 17th August 2022, which was rather fortuitous because it was the day before the 2nd anniversary of our webinar. The call was specifically to ask me for an update on the book on Ola Rotimi. I have aptly described the call, at various occasions, as serendipitous that can only be likened to a call from God, because it has succeeded in waking me up from my comatose. It is also worth putting on record for posterity that the VC, during the call, charged me that he wanted the book to be peer-reviewed, published and released by November 2022; and that I should update him on the progress of the book project on a weekly basis. Each time I updated the VC, regardless of the time of the night it was and no matter how busy he was, even if he was in a council meeting, he would find time to respond to my text. I am sure you understand now what I meant when I said in the opening paragraph of this introduction that but for the doggedness and can-do spirit of the Coach, this book would have remained a mere figment of my imagination rather than a tangible book in your hand or text on your screen that you are reading momentarily.

There is no doubt that, after his demise, a reasonable body of scholarship has been conducted into the life and artistic works of Ola Rotimi, particularly his significant contribution to the development and growth of popular theatre in Nigeria. In 2002, barely a couple of years after Rotimi's death, for instance, Effiok Uwatt's book, *Theatre of Feast: The Dramaturgy of Ola Rotimi,* was released by Sam Bookman Publishers. Uwatt is also the editor of *Playwriting and Directing in Nigeria: Interviews with Ola* Rotimi, which was published also in 2002 by Apex Books Limited. Another important book worth mentioning here is *The Theatre of Ola Rotimi: Power Politics and Postcolonialism* by Kemi Atanda Ilori, released in 2017 by Universal Books, UK. In terms of journal articles, Iyabode O. O Nwabuese's essay, 'Gender Equality: The Semantic Analysis of Ola Rotimi's *Our Husband Has Gone Mad Again',* which appeared in the *Journal of Pan African Studies*, readily comes to mind here. So is 'The Tragedy of History in Ola Rotimi's Oeuvres: A study of *Kurunmi* and *Ovonramwen Nogbaisi*' by Elija Olusegun which appeared in the *Academia* in 2018. In the same journal is another article entitled 'African Theatre, History and Postcolonial Resistance: An Appraisal of Ola Rotimi's *Ovonramwen Nogbaisi'* by Mubarak Ibrahim Lawan. Thus, while there's hardly a dearth of critical writings on Ola Rotimi, we believe that our book will further edge him in the consciousness of theatre practitioners as well as theatre lovers more than two decades after his demise.

This book has been loosely divided into two parts. The first part, 'The Multidimensionality of Ola Rotimi and His Theatre', begins with our very own Professor Akanji Nasiru's contribution, aptly entitled 'Contextualizing Ola Rotimi's Popular Theatre' in which he discusses how Ola Rotimi has created a niche for himself in the ecosystem of Nigerian theatre with his popular theatre. With due reference to relevant lines, particularly in *The Gods Are Not To Blame*, Nasiru's argument, *inter alia*, is that by domesticating the English language, Rotimi has succeeded in using the medium of theatre not to entertain but to communicate to all the strata of the Nigerian populace, irrespective of their educational backgrounds. From Nasiru, Prof Olu Obafemi collects the baton in chapter two, which is entitled 'History, Theatre language and Participation in the Political Process: The Theatre of Ola Rotimi'. In his own contribution, Obafemi takes us on a historical tour of the development of Rotimi's theatre with particular focus on its topicality and political dimension. Obafemi's submission is that rather than an art for art's sake, Rotimi's theatre is a commentary on

Nigeria's development and its political landscape. Then he expressed his deep gratitude to the webinar's organizers, participants and attendees.

In chapter three, Prof Julie Umukoro looks at how Ola Rotimi has, through his play, *Ovonramwen Nogbaisi,* contributed immensely to the better understanding of the rich tapestry and complexity of the Benin culture, particularly the awesomeness of the Oba of Benin. Prof Duro Oni, in chapter four, as evident in the title of his presentation (probably inspired by what Chief Emeka Odumegwu Ojukwu said about Chief Obafemi Awolowo), argues that Ola Rotimi was the best Artistic Director of the National Troupe that Nigeria never had. Oni's perspective is very important to be included in this volume for the record and posterity because, at the time he was the Special Adviser to the Minister of Culture to whom Ola Rotimi was recommended as the ideal candidate to take over the headship of the National Theatre from Hubert Ogunde who passed on to glory in 1990, having worked for four years as the artistic director of the National Troupe, which he was invited to set up in 1986. However, as you will see from reading Oni's chapter, the Minister was moved to another ministry and that was how Bayo Oduneye was appointed for the job. The interesting question Oni's chapter, raised, which no one but Ola Rotimi himself can answer is: would Rotimi have accepted the position were he to be offered?

Part two of the book opens with Peter Badejo's piece in which he tries to, from his personal experience of working with Ola Rotimi, fill the missing links of what Rotimi had actually contributed to the establishment and success of, what Badejo has referred to as, the Ori Olokun Experimental Workshop Project. It is some of the concerns Badejo raised in his concluding remark that are addressed in Emmanuel Nwachuku's piece which, as can be deduced from the title, 'Ola Rotimi the Playwright, Theatre Director and Lecturer: An Experiential Report', is based on his personal relationship with Ola Rotimi's family and his experience of studying under Rotimi as well as performing a number of lead roles in many of the stage productions of his and other people's plays. Then, in chapter seven, Bimbo Manuel similarly chronicles how he cuts his teeth in acting under the tutelage of Ola Rotimi at the University of Port Harcourt. Manuel's conclusion is that it was his personal experience with Ola Rotimi that has turned him to be the disciplined, focused, hardworking and ever busy theatre practitioner that he is known as today.

Having recently interviewed Austin Awulonu, who was a class mate of mine during my undergraduate days at Ife, for another book on Nigerian directors that

I am co-editing with Prof Duro Oni, I felt his passion for and kindred spirt with the great Ola Rotimi will be worth sharing in this book. Awulonu's contribution, 'Ola Rotimi: Ingenuity and Dexterity at Work' is the book's chapter eight and it is based, just like Nwachuku's piece, on Awulonu's close observation, when he was a directing undergraduate student at Obafemi Awolowo University in the late 80s, of Ola Rotimi at work. Without any doubt, Rotimi's dexterity, particularly, in handling crowd scenes on stage have greatly influenced Awulonu in the way he handles his own stage productions. Chapter nine of the book is a verbatim transcription of my interview with Prof Wole Soyinka, which as already indicated above, I played at the webinar as Soyinka's contribution to the event. In the interview, our own WS sheds light on his close working relationship with Ola Rotimi and how much he admired his deft directorial style, and with that single interview Kongi has finally dispelled the long-held rumour that he and Rotimi were rivals.

Enitan Rotimi, Ola Rotimi's first born, gave the vote of thanks to bring the webinar to a close on the day. Thus, to add a Rotimian touch to this book, I have asked him to send a copy of his closing remark on the day to me for it to be included in this book as its Afterword. In the piece, which I have taken the liberty to entitle, 'Our Dad: A Reader of Character and an Identifier of Creative Talents', as it came without any, Mr Enitan Rotimi Jr. expressed his gratitude to the attendees and organizers of the webinar before giving an insight into the kind of man his father was to both his biological children, as well as many whom he treated as his own children. He brought his remark to a close with the following words "...I thank you all once again for honoring our father on the twentieth anniversary of his passing and for keeping his name and works alive…Thanks again and God bless", which are most appropriate to bring this book to a close.

Thus, it is more or less how the webinar, which I also had the honour of moderating, started and ended that I have structured this book. With gratitude to God and His favoured servant on earth in the person of Prof Joshua Ogunwole, I am extremely proud to present to you *Remembering Ola Rotimi: A Complete Man of the Theatre.* It is my hope that by making it possible for this book to hit the book shelves two years after the webinar, The Coach and all of us in the College of Liberal Studies and, particularly, in the Theatre Arts Programme of Bowen University, Iwo, have succeeded in contributing our small quota in ensuring that, though gone forever, Ola Rotimi's memory continues to live on and linger in our hearts, minds and souls forever and ever more.

# PART I

# The Multidimensionality of Ola Rotimi and His Theatre

# CHAPTER ONE

## Contextualizing Ola Rotimi's Popular Theatre

*Akanji Nasiru*

### Introduction

Having had the benefit of observing about a decade of the nascent Nigerian theatre and the criticism of it, Ola Rotimi quickly enunciated his preference for a popular theatre that would appeal to a wide range of the Nigerian audience. Towards this end, his primary focus was to domesticate the English language in his plays so as to reach out to the intelligentsia as well as the preponderant semi-literate Nigerian population. This deliberate toning down of the language was both novel and entertaining, but its downside included the criticism that his watered-down language was not always in consonance with the serious subjects he explored and the messages he intended to convey to his audience. His later plays would demonstrate a modification of this initial approach while he still maintained his primary objective to communicate with a wide range of Nigerian speakers of the English language. But beyond his fascination with language, there were other important dimensions to his popular theatre. They included his consistent exploration of well-known stories – myths as well as history – as vehicles for dialoguing with his primary audience on issues of national importance, his exciting and dynamic staging technique, and his acceptance of the challenge of taking the theatre to the people in structures accessible and acceptable to them. This chapter contextualizes Rotimi's popular theatre with a particular focus on how it has bequeathed to Nigerian theatre and the younger generation of Nigerian dramatists a legacy of conscious, audience-centred experimentation that has helped to gain a wider audience for drama of English expression.

### Situating Ola Rotimi Historically

By reason of age, Ola Rotimi is among the first generation of Nigerian dramatists of English expression. If he were alive today, he would be eighty-four years old. By comparison, J. P. Clark was eighty-five when he passed on in 2020, and Wole Soyinka is now eighty-eight. Therefore, we are talking of

Nigerian dramatists all of whom were born in the 1930s. In reality, however, Rotimi arrived on the Nigerian stage nearly ten years after those two notable dramatists. *The Gods Are Not to Blame*, which marked his debut, was first staged in 1968. Compare that to Wole Soyinka's *The Swamp Dwellers* (1958), *The Lion and the Jewel* (1959), and *A Dance of the Forests* (1960), or to Clark's *Song of a Goat* (1961). The point to note here is that Rotimi had the benefit of ten years of his precursors' practice and the criticism that their works received, which was of immense value to their individual growth and development as dramatists. It also had great implications for the growth of Nigerian drama and literature in general. Add to that the fact that the sixties were marked by vigorous discussions of African literature in general and drama in particular, and one arrives at the inescapable conclusion that Ola Rotimi stepped into Nigeria and Africa's dramatic arena well aware of the major issues at stake and the challenges before him as a dramatist.

The sixties was a period when important questions were being asked of African writings in foreign languages and their implications for the growth of the continent's literature and drama. Chief among those questions were those involving the writer's chosen language vis-a-vis his intended audience. In choosing to write in a foreign language, who was the African writer writing for? Whose voice did he represent, and to whom was he speaking and sending his message? The sixties also saw a rapid socio-political transformation of the continent of Africa occasioned especially by the attainment of self-rule by roughly half of the countries that had been ruled by European governments for many decades. Literature was perceived by critics and the writers themselves, and quite rightly too, as an important tool for the representation of Africa to the world, but even more importantly – to Africans themselves. It was expected to be a beacon to shape opinions and guide policies towards a better Africa that would fulfil the hopes and aspirations of a people long exploited and subjugated. In this regard, drama carried a greater social responsibility, being an art form that brings the artist and his audience together in a manner that has potential for immediacy of communication and possibility of direct results arising from this unique interaction of performance and audience.

Ola Rotimi knew all that, nor could he have missed the fervour with which writers and critics sometimes expressed their convictions at their gatherings and in various publications. For example, the dire prognosis made for the new African literature by the critic Obi Wali is evident in the provocative title of his 1963 article, 'The Dead End of African Literature', in which he argued that African writing in the European languages, in his opinion,

> is severely limited to the European-oriented, few college graduates in the new Universities of Africa, steeped as they are in European literature and culture. The ordinary local audience, with little or no education in the conventional European manner, and who constitute an overwhelming majority has no chance of participating in this kind of literature. (Wali 1963, 14)

Writing four years later, Oladele Taiwo was less strident, but his judgment was similarly critical of the adoption of a foreign language by an African writer: "Language is one of the four reasons why drama in English has failed to appeal to a wider audience in Nigeria" (1967, 73-74). Such criticism must have prompted Ola Rotimi to formulate one of the guiding principles of his dramaturgy, of which language would become cardinal. The deliberate choice he made in this regard is key to a full appreciation of his drama, for it is one of the distinguishing characteristics of his approach to create a drama that would have a popular appeal.

## Language as a Significant Factor in Rotimi's Popular Drama

Language quickly became a major factor in Rotimi's drama. In particular, the unique brand of English that he consciously fashioned would become his distinctive signature, bringing a fresh dimension to the Nigerian stage. His preoccupation was to create a type of English that would reach out and yield meaning to persons who have a wide range of proficiency in the language. His manifesto is made clear in an interview published in *Dem-Say, Interviews with Eight Nigerian Writers* edited by Bernth Lindfors:

> English . . . is the official medium of communication in Nigeria, However, in handling the English language in my plays, I strive to temper its phraseology to the ear of both dominant semi- literate as well as the literate classes, ensuring that my dialogue reaches out to both groups with ease in assimilation and clarity in identification. (Lindfors 1974, 60)

Rotimi's language more than reached out; it held a special appeal to an audience that had long been used to correct, formal, and even poetic English issuing out of the mouths of leading characters in many Nigerian and African plays. To hear Odewale say "madness is in your liver" or Aderopo retort "your head is not well" (Rotimi 2013, 32) was to hear sentiments that were familiar enough, but the manner of expression was what made for the novelty. Rotimi was in effect "seasoning" the English language with distinctly Nigerian spices, an approach for which Dapo Adelugba, a well-known critic, would later coin the word "Yorubanglish", which he defines as,

> Not just Yoruba English or Yoruba mixed with English but the many-sided attempts to catch the flavor, tones, rhythms, emotional and intellectual content of Yoruba language and thought in an adventurous brand of English. (Adelugba 1978, 216)

Because Rotimi's deliberate linguistic choices often relied on what appeared like simplistic, word-bound translations of familiar Yoruba expressions, he was initially criticized by Adelugba as descending into "patois" and "bathos" and "banalities" (Adelugba 1969, 49), but there could be no doubt that the playwright achieved the popularity that he desired for his drama, as was evident from the size of the audience he attracted. On and off campus, people flocked to the performance of the plays of this new entrant to the Nigerian stage who quickly acquired a reputation for rich humour, especially on account of the English language of his plays. They knew they would be treated to a rich serving of English with local "seasoning", of which copious examples can be found also in his subsequent plays, *Kurunmi* and *Our Husband Has Gone Mad Again*. And this was precisely why he attracted large audiences.

But there was far more to his language than quaint renditions of Yoruba proverbs and stock expressions. For one thing, he could, when he chose to, take the trouble to effect translations that retain the profundity of the original expressions, as the following two examples show:

> When the frog in front falls into a pit, others behind take caution… When crocodiles eat their own eggs, what will they not do to the flesh of a frog? (Rotimi 1971, 48)

There are in the above examples no quaint renditions, no trivialization of the subject in a deliberate bid to draw laughter from the audience. Indeed, Rotimi's subsequent plays reveal that he had learnt the lesson that there is an extent to which a literary artist can compromise over his choice of language. Whatever popular advantages it may serve, concessions to an audience's level of proficiency in a particular language may not always be in the interest of the playwright's craft. They could detract from the profundity of the thought and message he wishes to pass across to his audience, and that ultimately takes much away from the overall quality of the work. *Ovoramwen Nogbaisi*, for example, is in part distinctively poetic, matching the lofty grandeur of the exalted protagonist, a monarch whose tragic fall also signifies the subjugation of a notable African empire by a superior foreign power. Similarly, the protagonists of *If...* and *Hopes of the Living Dead*, both plays of profound sociopolitical import for contemporary Nigeria, do not indulge in the "Do not open your noses at me" (Rotimi 1971, 13) kind of linguistic register that draws from an audience laughter that is incongruous to the serious situations depicted in *The Gods Are Not to Blame*.

The simple but profound lesson that the playwright seemed to have learnt is that in choosing a language for one's thought, one is in effect choosing an audience for one's message, and only those who have a reasonable level of proficiency in the language can benefit fully from the totality of the effect that the work is meant to convey to the audience. In the same vein, it should be assumed that a person who goes to the theatre to see a play (or picks up a play text) written in English already has the level of competence that guarantees that he will make meaning and derive enjoyment from his encounter with the work. In an early study of the English language in the works of some Nigerian playwrights, we had proposed that level of competence as that attainable by an average middle-former in a Nigerian secondary school. Our argument is based on the fact that that is the stage when students are competent enough in the English language to embark on the study of specialized subjects like Biology, Chemistry, Physics, Economics, Government and English Literature, and to begin work on the School Certificate syllabus (see Nasiru 1978, 32 and 39).

It is also pertinent to mention here that it is curious that Rotimi's search for a simplified form of English did not suggest to him the possibility of Nigerian pidgin English, which had for long been a kind of *lingua franca* spoken by elements from different linguistic and ethnic backgrounds, especially those living, working and trading in the major cities of Nigeria, particularly in the southern parts. When he finally gave attention to pidgin, Rotimi like many other playwrights before him was only interested in the language for dramatic purposes (especially to delineate characters of lowly status). But Rotimi's initial preoccupation with domesticating the English language for the benefit of his Nigerian audience is by no means the single or most important aspect of his theatre. It is important to give equal attention to a few other aspects of his dramaturgy that contribute to their popular appeal.

## The Primacy of Story

A consummate storyteller, Ola Rotimi places premium on a good story as a means of capturing and sustaining the attention of his audience. In his words,

> I try to anchor my play to a vivid story line…The African culture is one that has a great attachment to stories. And to hold (your audience's) interest your story must be sound. (Lindfors 1974, 60)

This may be one reason why a good number of his plays are dramatizations of well-known mythical and historical narratives. In *The Gods Are Not to Blame,* he transposes the ancient Greek myth of King Oedipus into a Yoruba setting, making his King Odewale the tragic victim of fate as well as his own irascible nature. In both *Kurunmi* and *Ovoramwen Nogbaisi*, he explores for tragic effect the lives of two Nigerian monarchs who are compelled by circumstances to make choices that eventually have tragic consequences they could not have foreseen. In *Hopes of the Living Dead,* he depicts the heroic struggle of Harcourt Whyte, a gifted musician who overcame leprosy and organized the Lepers' Rebellion of 1928-32 so as to save himself and his marginalized fellow lepers. In *Akassa You Mi* (2001), he dramatizes the war waged in 1895 by the people of Nembe, under King Fredrick Koko, against the Royal Niger Company in an attempt to stop the British usurpation and monopolization of trade in the area.

In each of those mythical and historical narratives, Rotimi finds appropriate material to demonstrate a pet idea of his: what constitutes heroic action in human life. As he stated in 1972, the hero is "someone who upholds a principle or conviction in the face of crisis, fully cognizant of the possibilities of being overwhelmed in the act" (Rotimi 1972, 6). As often happens in such situations, the hero is, indeed, overwhelmed, which then makes him a tragic hero, as in the examples of Odewale, Ovonramwen and Kurunmi. However, he is overwhelmed but not humiliated, for he has become, by virtue of the moral choice he makes, a representative of the very best of the human spirit, struggling in the face of great odds. The respect we have for him transcends the feeling of pity that we must necessarily feel for any suffering character; it is an expression of our belief in the essential nobility of the human spirit. Thus, even at the moment of his fall, the tragic hero is exalted rather than derided or scorned.

But in *Hopes of the Living Dead*, we can joyfully celebrate this nobility as we witness the denouement of the heroic struggle, with Harcourt Whyte and his band having achieved the respect and dignity that is rightfully theirs. What emerges from all this is that Rotimi's exploration of these stories goes beyond the urge to merely render a fascinating story in dramatic form. His popular drama comes with a strong sense of the responsibility of the artist to his society. He strives to fulfil the universally accepted mantra that art at its best not only entertains but also instructs its audience in a broad sense, challenging them to higher and nobler causes that are the means by which the human society advances.

## Rotimi's Total Theatre

Beyond linguistic and literary concerns, the uniqueness of the theatre lies in those modes of communication that may not be so obvious to a casual reader of a play script. Stage directions often accompany the lines to be spoken by characters, and glossing over them may lead to an inadequate or even wrong understanding of the full meaning intended by the playwright. Actors' gestures and movements complement the spoken word in ways that enrich an understanding of the deeper meanings embedded in a piece of action. Songs and chants communicate not only through their words, but also through the equally important moods that they convey to a theatre rather than a reading audience. All these elements constitute what has always been regarded as the larger language of the theatre: they contribute to the overall meaning of a play and its effect on an audience. Theatre in the African culture is unique because it relies for full effect on an exploration of various communication modes, in the spirit of what is known as 'total theatre', "a type of performing arts that incorporates multiple art forms to create a complete and immersive experience for the audience" (see 'The History And Importance of Total Theatre'), and Ola Rotimi demonstrated from the outset that he is a master of that form.

*The Gods* opens with mimed action, very quickly progresses into a mini festival as a whole community celebrates the arrival of a new life in singing and dancing. There is a problem in the land, but the charisma of the King leads the community to express their faith and optimism in another dance sequence. Then the Royal Bard steps on stage to eulogize the King and Queen in a short but stylized performance. Throughout the play, the action is punctuated at critical junctures with songs, chants and stylized movements. It is difficult to imagine a new dramatist bursting on the Nigerian stage in a more captivating manner. Here again, we must emphasize that Rotimi has not gratuitously employed these various modes for cheap effect. Rather, he often uses them as an integral part of the meaning and mood of the play. A single instance will suffice to make this point. At the beginning of Act Two Scene 3, Queen Ojuola leads the children of the palace in singing the "Olurombi" song after telling them a folk tale. The session on the surface looks like a naturalistic depiction of an idyllic, rustic life. But the audience has just heard an angry King Odewale utter in annoyance the words, "May my eyes not see Aderopo again till I die" (Rotimi 1971, 35) – ominous words spoken in anger that will turn out to be prophetic in a manner the character does not intend. The playwright deliberately juxtaposes that previous scene with this song of a woman who had earlier made a rather audacious promise to give to the Iroko spirit anything that it would demand if it would grant her huge profit in her trade. The spirit grants her prayer but now demands nothing but the woman's only daughter in return for its benevolence. The implication is clear: like the woman, Olurombi, Odewale has made a rash pledge that he will greatly rue later. Here, Rotimi has employed familiar story from Yoruba folklore to reinforce meaning in the overall tragic context of the play.

*Ovonramwen Nogbaisi* features Ola Rotimi's total theatre in a very profound manner. His copious use of music, chant and choreographed movement effectively evokes the tragic mood of the play, which also depicts the fall of the reigning monarch as well as that of the Benin Empire. Battle scenes can be very challenging for a director to depict on stage, and it would be monotonous to attempt to capture the many key moments of the military conflict between Edo forces and the British army. The brilliant method that the playwright adopts is to depict once and for all, and through symbolic action, the encounter of the two military forces:

> British martial music again; subliminal Benin war drums. Consul- General Moore appears, bearing the British flag flown from a medium-length pole. He advances towards Ologbosere who steps forward also – the two approaching centre-stage. Getting there, they both stop, some two yards apart. Low lights on Oba Ovonramwen watching the imminent confrontation.
>
> For a brief while, Moore and Ologbosere stand glaring at each other. Then, first slowly, the movement building up, they begin to stalk each other; feline malevolence. Suddenly, they attack – the stems of their national symbols strike together, and lock. Pressure is applied on both sides, for a while, a stalemate . . . then oscillation, as the one strains to weigh down the other. At last . . . gradually, painfully, Ologbosere begins

to give ground – sinking lower and lower under the oppressive muscles of his opponent.

British martial music swells forth, drowning the already dying beats of Benin war drums. Booms of cannon- fire from the British artillery, offstage. In that instant, Moor's soldiers – predominantly blacks led by British officers – pour on stage from all directions with a deafening huzzah, wildly brandishing flaming torches. Ologbosere ducks and takes to his heels, Moor in hot pursuit, his soldiers following victoriously. (Rotimi 1974, 43)

In fact, Rotimi's dramaturgy in the play relies almost in equal parts on dialogue as much as music, chants and choreography. In this regard, it is pertinent to mention that his theatre benefited greatly from his work at the Institute of African Studies at the then University of Ife. Present at the Institute were fellow senior researchers in various fields – History, Music, Choreography and Fine Arts – whose works were available for him to explore in his plays. His fascination with history, which we earlier noted, is obviously one of the gains of his contact with the works of fellow researchers; it is one of those areas that he explored over and over again in his plays, including in the vital areas of his historically accurate costume and stage setting. The influence of the famous choreographer, Peggy Harper, also a researcher at the Institute, was often evident in the impressively choreographed movement and crowd scenes in his plays. All these factors combined to make his productions appeal greatly to his audiences.

## A Diligent Seeker of the Popular Audience

Ola Rotimi did not just put into his drama the ingredients that he knew would appeal to a popular audience, he also diligently sought that audience out at the kind of venues and structures where he knew they would feel at home. Early Nigerian drama in English was in most cases a campus affair, written by members of the intelligentsia, especially persons who had their training in the liberal arts and were familiar with world literary classics, philosophical thought and critical tenets. That background influenced their writing style and staging conventions. Inevitably, they catered for the taste of the primary audience they knew so well and were part of, including the critics who would pronounce judgment on their works. At the University of Ibadan, for example, serious drama was invariably staged at the Arts Theatre, whether by on-campus groups (usually staff and students) or by similar groups visiting from sister universities such as Ife and Lagos. The indigenous theatre troupes (led by dramatists like Hubert Ogunde, Duro Ladipo and Kola Ogunmola, all of them household names among popular theatre lovers) were more likely to prefer the more spacious, general-purpose Trenchard Hall or the courtyard of the Institute of African Studies. The artificial dichotomy between popular and "serious" (highbrow) theatre was thus reflected in the venues where the performances took place.

Ola Rotimi started to break down the artificial barrier between the two types of theatre when he deliberately chose to take his plays outside the familiar and regular theatre venues to the unconventional ones like the Ife University stadium, or the spacious courtyard of the Institute of African Studies at the University of Ibadan. In Ile Ife town, his Ori Olokun Theatre acquired a space in Arubidi quarters deep in the town for its rehearsals and performances. This was a very shrewd move for two reasons. First, since most members of his troupe were junior level artistes and artisans who lived in town, working at that venue saved his productions precious funds, for it was much cheaper to move the relatively smaller number of staff and student members from the campus to that venue rather than the other way round. Secondly, the troupe's presence and activities in that locality soon began to attract large crowds of town folks who craved entertainment, thereby creating for the troupe a growing followership of town theatregoers.

## Conclusion: Ola Rotimi's Influence

Ola Rotimi's significant contribution to the Nigerian theatre is his courageous exploration of a kind of English that would easily communicate with and appeal to a wide range of Nigerian speakers of the English language – the highly educated staff and students that could be found on university campuses, the much larger population of public servants, teachers and schoolchildren, and even the multifarious mix of factory workers, self-employed artisans and labourers that make up most Nigerian urban communities. Along with this linguistic exploration, he relied on a heavy infusion of popular performance modes from the indigenous tradition, giving his theatre a total theatre flavour that appeals to the masses of the people. Equally important is that he took his theatre to venues and structures where he knew he would find a popular audience.

Admittedly, some of the features of Ola Rotimi's theatre that we have highlighted above may not have been exclusive to him; but their combination and his consistent pursuit of them, in play after play, made him stand out as a new and refreshingly different dramatist in those early years of the development of Nigerian drama in English. This unique approach gave a fillip to a conscious drive for a popular form of theatre of English expression on the part of a younger generation of dramatists who now began to see virtue in tuning their craft towards a much wider audience than the drama had hitherto captured. Some of them were university-trained performers who chose to set up their practice in particular communities, such as Segun Taiwo, who in 1985 set up his Ayota Theatre in Ajegunle, a suburb of Lagos. Taiwo's productions relied on the popular music and dance of the people to communicate with them. Funsho Alabi, who trained at the then University of Ife and once taught at the University of Lagos, went on to specialise in one-man performances that addressed the new social and health problems, such as AIDS and drug abuse. With support from the United States Information Service (USIS), he toured university campuses as well as secondary schools, using popular theatre methods to sensitise Nigerian youths to the growing problems and encouraging them to embrace a healthy and responsible lifestyle. Sadly, both theatre artists passed away in their prime.

Happily, however, a growing body of plays, some of them now published, attest to the fervour with which many young dramatists have embraced the popular theatre tradition. Beginning from the early eighties, the evidence was there to see in the rich theatre culture springing up all over the country. Not surprisingly, the formal study of drama in higher institutions began to give recognition to the new theatre culture. Nowadays, performing arts is prominent in the curricula of most drama and theatre departments, with equal attention being given to indigenous performance modes. The National Universities Commission (NUC) benchmark for theatre programmes also includes Community Theatre, thus making popular theatre an integral focus of the training of the new generation of theatre students. These are all a testimony to the fire lit by Ola Rotimi about half a century ago. They constitute the legacy that he bequeathed to theatre and theatre studies in Nigeria.

## References

Adelugba, Dapo. October 1969. 'Theatre Critique'. *Ibadan.* No. 27. 49-50.

Adelugba, Dapo. 1978. 'Three Dramatists in Search of a Language. *Theatre in Africa* (eds.) Ogunba, Oyin and Abiola Irele. 201-220.

Lindfors, Bernth (ed.). 1974. *Dem-Say, Interviews with Eight Nigerian Writers,* African and Afro-American Research Institute, The University of Texas, Austin.

Nasiru, Akanji. 1978. 'Communication and the Nigerian Drama in English'. Unpublished Ph.D. Thesis, University of Ibadan.

Rotimi, Ola. 1971. *The Gods Are Not to Blame.* Oxford University Press, Ibadan.

_________ 1972. 'A Definition of the Tragic Hero.' Unpublished paper presented at a workshop on playwriting. University of Ife.

_________ 1974. *Ovonramwen Nogbaisi.* Ethiope Publishing Corporation/Oxford University Press, Ibadan.

_________ 1988. *Hopes of the Living Dead.* Spectrum Books, Ibadan.

_________ 2001. *Akassa You Mi.* University of Port Harcourt Press.

Taiwo, Oladele. 1967. *An Introduction to West African Literature.* Thomas Nelson and Sons Ltd. 73-75.

# CHAPTER TWO

## History, Theatre Language and Participation in the Political Process: The Theatre of Ola Rotimi

*Olu Obafemi*

### Introduction

The very fact that, more than twenty years after his untimely demise, barely sixty years old, Ola Rotimi is being put on the remembrance stage through this volume, eloquently testifies to the immortal significance of this great theatre maker to the humanities. In reminiscence of my physical and intellectual encounters with the subject of discourse and celebration, I recall three land-marking events.

First. In the year 1975, as a young man and a National Youth Service Corps teacher in the East Central State of Nigeria (now Anambra State among the four states carved out of it), I produced Rotimi's *The God's Are Not To Blame.* The production of the play had been a dream come true. Since I watched the play in one of the Halls of the Ahmadu Bello University as an undergraduate student in 1973, I believe, and the emotional impact of the play on me and the entire audience, the nudge to produce the play had been a burden until this realization of the play on stage. Being an all-Boys School, (Okongwu Memorial Secondary School, Nnewi, a stone throw from Odumegwu Ojukwu's home) I deployed an all-male crew and cast for the production which I toured round many of the major towns of the State—Owerri, Onitsha, Awonmama, Enugu, Ihiala, Aguata and so on—to very appreciative audiences.

Second. On June 26, 1991, I was in attendance at Ola Rotimi's Inaugural Lecture, in the company of Prof Femi Osofisan, with whom I had traveled all the way from Ibadan the previous night just to share in the joy of the intellectual event. Having done some study of his plays, including writing a whole chapter on his two most significant tragi-historical plays, *Kurunmi* and *Ovonramwen Nogbaisi*, besides reading a few of his essays, I had never had the opportunity to partake in the intellectual engagements of the great man of the stage. The very enthralling lecture, cryptically titled 'African Dramatic Literature: To be or To Become' was rounded off with an evening of rich, variegated entertainments.

Thirdly, there was the somber and sobering experience of finding myself at his graveside, again in the company of Femi Osofisan when he joined his ancestors, twenty years ago. We had been in Ile-Ife, on the invitation of the great musician-actor, Jimi Solanke, who had put an event together in honour of Wole Soyinka, only to be told very early in the morning, that Ola Rotimi had slept and left the world in the middle of his sleep.

These three experiences impacted strongly on my intellectual and theatrical experience on and around the great impish giant of the stage: Gladstone Olawale Rotimi. I shall limit this intellectual recourse to his work on what I perceive as the hardly engaged aspect of his work—the political dimension of his dramatic art, the route he followed to make his intervention in the political landmines of our troubled and traumatized nation and how he has made his theatre a platform of mediation on Nigeria's political terrain.

## Biodata and Major Plays of Ola Rotimi

Ordinarily, it would be too trivial to engage in any detailed recount of his life story, works and theatre life, which could easily be picked from the internet or any serious study of Ola Rotimi. Master Google has eased our task in this dimension. But in context, it bears restating, since there are a few confusing renderings of his early life history. Rotimi was born on April 13, 1938 in Sapele, Delta State of Nigeria, to an Ijaw mother and a Yoruba father. He schooled at Methodist High School Lagos, the College of Arts, Boston and Yale Universities in the United States. He taught and worked on the stage in the United States of America before returning home to Nigeria on a Research Foundation, first to the University of Ife, Ile-Ife, where he played a pivotal role in the founding of the Ori Olokun Acting Company later rechristened Ori Olokun Players. In 1977, Rotimi proceeded to the University of Port Harcourt where he held a position of a Professor in Theatre Arts. In both experiences, Ola Rotimi wielded tremendous impact on the theatre life of Nigeria as one of the most rounded, talented and prominent, experimental directors on the Nigerian stage and notable playwright, who recoursed to traditional performance aesthetic and architecture for his theatre activism.

The first extant play of Rotimi is *To Stir the God of Iron* which he wrote in 1963 when he was twenty-five. Three years later, his play, *Our Husband Has Gone Mad Again,* was directed for the stage in America by Jack Landau. It is an indication of the times the play was written that it was not published until 1977, long after Rotimi had firmly established himself as a formidable presence in the Nigerian theatre. *Our Husband* marked Rotimi's entry into political theatre. It was set in a fictitious General Election that is recognisably Nigeria.

Lejoka Brown, the protagonist, combines a career as a military officer with being a prosperous cocoa merchant, and who launches himself into party politics with the hope and expectation of making money. To contribute to the possibilities for comic confusion is the fact that Lejoka Brown has two Nigerian wives and an expatriate wife who suddenly surfaces at the height of election. *Our Husband* is a robust entertainment in which the political is mixed with the domestic. It is written in standard English laced with pidgin that contributes to the comedy.

In some respects, that 1966 play anticipates Rotimi's later work, *If: A Tragedy of the Ruled*, that was staged in Ile-Ife in 1979, in the middle of actual General Elections, during the Second Republic in Nigeria. Again, there was a delay in publication and *If*, written from the perspective of the proletariat—the working class in the oppressive and predatory grips of their landlord—was published in 1983. The play graphically depicts the playwright's disillusionment with the corrupt political elite. In terms of dramaturgy, and theatricality, the play reveals ample melodramatic features. They are realized in music which is deployed to heighten the tragic flavour and tone of the play.

*The Gods Are Not to Blame* marks Rotimi's foray into intertextual drama—the recreation of another text through adaptation. Sophocles' *Oedipus Rex* is the exploited text for the creation of *The Gods.* The premiere of the play in 1968 was also the launch of the Olori Olokun Acting Company. As with *Our Husband,* the play, published in 1971, carries a heavy political undertone and it is significant that it was produced as the Nigerian Civil War was raging.

Rotimi shifts the focus of the play from preternatural forces (the Gods); the tragic flaw of the protagonist, Odewale, and laid at the doorstep of the sub-national, ethnic politics and loyalties that featured dominantly in the politics of the First Republic, which is both the *casus belli* of the Civil War and a thematic locus of the play itself. The dramatic essence of the play is its inter-textuality, the adaptation of an ancient text, with recreative interpretation through an adaptation. *The Gods* is an adaptation of Sophocles' *Oedipus Rex*, resting the protagonist's tragic flaw, not solely (if at all, because the oedipal consciousness still looms large in the play, in spite of the playwright's conscious downplay of that theme) on the Greek theme.

The question of inter-ethnic loyalty, which was a major factor in the Nigerian civil war, became the focus of the play. Note that the loyalty of the chief character, Odewale, was more intra than inter-ethnic, since both he and the stranger (his father whom he took for a stranger are of the same tribal stock, with mere dialectal variance) who he killed for mocking his tongue. In other words, Rotimi, from a strong political viewpoint, considered the tragedy of Odewale, the protagonist, as the result of his own uncritical tribal sentiment as well as the failure of government – the failed leadership of the African political elite – a perception which exonerates the metaphysical forces from the tragic fall of the protagonist and Africa's political crisis.

This corresponds with Ola Rotimi's concern that theatre should participate in the political destiny of a nation—a concern that has begun to emerge in *The Gods Are Not to Blame.* This pertains to the need to urgently be involved in the national project of becoming; and for art to point the direction in which the nation should go. This, in a sense, reveals the playwright's concern that theatre should form part of the national culture as both economic base and superstructure—a nudging of theatre to become integral to national discourse and envisioning process by engaging in the issues of designing the political stability, economic vibrancy, self- reliance, self-worth and renewal of the nation-state. Odewale's provocation to violence on account of ethnic loyalty and sensitivity— "he abused my tribe" as a justification for murderous violence— projects this view of the rabid macro-ethnic reconstruction of the federating nexus, the on-going regrouping process where conviction is centred around primordial factors (ethnic identities), which had since become a critical factor since the civil war. In other words, the notion of and obsession with carving up/balkanizing our national space, christened in various configuring perspectives as restructuring and in extreme circumstances, toward self-determination and insurrection. You can extend this to the historical plays—*Kurunmi and Ovonramwen Nogbaisi.*

*Kurunmi* (1969), for instance, is usually read as a deployment of history to project a tragic vision (see: Obafemi 1996 and 2000). This is the reading of the protagonist ego as built around a tragic hero, Aare Kurunmi. This tragico-historical interpretation is a depiction of the intra-ethnic, internecine wars among the Yoruba in the mid-19th century. But we should observe that the play was written during the Civil War. Rotimi himself recalled that he was caught unawares by the reactions of the audience during production, as he did not relate the play directly to the war. He was of course, in his confession, aware of the prevailing situation in the country then, – in terms of the civil war, but he stated that he did not "studiously relate the play to it" (Folarin 2002, 77). I find this very difficult to swallow, writing and producing a play during a national carnage and feeling totally oblivious of the effect it could have on the real and stage production in a war situation; especially given the proximal referents of the stage characters and the real war personages of the war being prosecuted at hand, beats the imagination. The sensitive audience began to nickname characters in the play, based on their actions and utterances in relation to the reportage of 'the actions and utterances' of prominent Nigerians and warriors at the then current warfront. This again typifies the immediate political relevance of the play to the national situation – the immediate political impact of the script/stage performance on the social order and disorder.

*Ovonramwen Nogbaisi* is an enactment of the so-called punitive expedition of the British against the Benin Empire, through extreme display by the British imperialists of ideological and cultural contempt for Africans and vandalism of Africa's invaluable material wealth. They had come to impoverish people and perpetuate untold pogrom on the Benin people. The play was unequivocal about the cultural genocide being perpetrated by the British in the so-called punitive expedition (economic and cultural lootage in fact) of 1897, in which the Benin people were massacred, their monarch humiliated and exiled and their invaluable and priceless artifacts pillaged.

All these earlier plays were foreboding and anticipatory of the larger dramatic canvas of Rotimi's politics resulting from his artistic/dramatic engagements—the evolution of his democratic theatre from the perspective of the lumpen proletariat and the downtrodden of society, which began to manifest, unobtrusively, from *If: A Tragedy of the Ruled* (1979) as well as *Holding Talks: An Absurdist Drama.* As already hinted earlier, *If...* was actually staged in the middle of the real General Election of Nigeria's Second Republic of 1979, conducted by the military government of General Olusegun Obasanjo. The play was later published in 1983, toward the eve of another military interregnum. It is least surprising, if one takes cognizance of my interpretation of the political consciousness of the playwright already manifest in the earlier plays, that the play was written from the standpoint of the lumpen proletarian and peasant class—the oppressed masses, presently being predated upon by the symbol of the bourgeoisie, represented by the landlord who was seeking political power through the liberal democratic system that would soon be discredited by a returning military dictatorship. The play is again some crystal-ball clairvoyant portent of the incipient anger of the citizens, which the military will soon cash in upon, as seen in the jubilant explosion in the streets as the military later announced its seizure of the reins of government.

*If: A Tragedy of the Ruled* thus launches us into the democratic phase of Rotimi's dramaturgy. It is a loose adaptation of the Trinidadian Errol John's 1957 play, *Moon on a Rainbow Shawl* and captures and contains a spirit of collectivism that we shall fully encounter in Rotimi's most revolutionary play, *Hopes of the Living Dead.* The latter play is based on Ikoli Harcourt-Whyte's struggle and seminal experience as a leper from teenage (19 years). Leprosy, as we know, is a communicable, contagious but curable disease. The play was deployed, in Niyi Osundare's words, as "grand metaphor for a social, political and psychological disease, which though daunting and stigmatising can be tackled" (qtd. in Banham 1988, 843) as Harcourt-Whyte did in the play in which he leads a revolution of kindred spirits for revolutionary purposes against the predation.

In *Hopes,* more than in his earlier plays, Ola Rotimi utilizes the democratic nature of oral performance as a dialectical art to evoke a democratic social discourse. This is done largely through a multi-media theatre language, idiom and dramaturgy by employing the indigenous theatre resource of music, kinesics, gesture, mimesis, chant and dialogue (devices which we require a full-length discussion to fully access) from numerous Nigerian languages to emphasize the collectivist vision and the solidarity of the oppressed as a weapon of social and political struggle. In doing this, the total theatre format and the creation of communal spectacle for human condition discourse were masterfully and craft-fully deployed in this play and other Ola Rotimi's plays. Even in as early as *The Gods,* communal spectacle and populist staging account for the essential theatricality of the play. *Hopes* explores the issue of class stratification and the antagonistic relationship between hegemonists and the proletariat, the unemployed and unemployable downtrodden citizens, especially the physically challenged such as the lepers in that colony.

On the level of language, I believe that, many years after Rotimi's demise, *Hopes* is still, arguably, the most experimental, most theatrically adventurous on the Nigerian stage—in its utilization of many indigenous Nigerian languages, nearly as originally and as naturally spoken by Rotimi's diverse, multi-ethnic, multi-linguistic actors. It comes out in dramatic polylogue to advance the democratic imperative of socio-communal struggle as anticipated by the playwright's ideological bent. In this frame, Femi Osofisan has earlier and graphically described Rotimi as the only Nigerian dramatist who could make such a "successful use of plural tongues and simultaneous translations with the formula of each-one-tell-one" (2016, 164). This is tantamount to a democratization of the linguistic process to articulate a democratic social vision. The playwright breaks through the usually politically erected barriers of linguistic diversity to propose a dialectic of social transformation. This play is probably the acme of the stage realization of Rotimi's political theatre. It must be said, of course, it is not the height of his ambition with theatrical adventure and expectation.

There are other Rotimi's plays with this trend, with less remarkable levels of success, in spite of his continued experimentation with the stage. *When the Criminals Become Judges* (1995) is one instance. There are also the two unpublished plays - *The Epilogue* and *Man Talk, Woman Talk,* which is a typical Rotimian slapstick humour—without the literal wefting of pieces of wood which, in the original concept, clowns deployed to effectuate ribald—the essence of the incongruous actions for comic fare. In this instance, a womanist intent is the aim. But this is not a provocation of gender antagonism or a superiority tussle among the sexes. Rotimi deploys the concept within the womanist concept of accommodation, the complementarity of the genders to explore their specific strengths to build robust humanity. A recently directed version of the play by Bimbo Olorunyomi at the Ace-Olivia, City Mall, Onikan, Lagos, is close to the realization of slapstick comedy to demystify the usual staging of the patriarchal notion, with a persuasive and compelling political vision intended by the playwright.

We have tried so far to project and explore, to a certain level, Rotimi's theatre of political purpose which we have attempted to canvass in this essay.

## The Theatre Language of Rotimi's Politics

On the issue of Rotimi's theatre language and its mechanics to articulate this political vision, many scholars have made extensive perceptive inroads into his remarkable effort. Such pioneer critics of his theatre, including Martin Banham, Dapo Adelugba, Bode Sowande, Akanji Nasiru, Olu Obafemi, and so on, have, in their various perspectives, identified his experimentation with language for the stage. It will amount to an exercise in tedium to elaborate in any extensive way some of the perceptive discourses of Rotimi's innovative theatre language here.

Only a few instances will suffice to clarify the trend. Dapo Adelugba, a prominent Nigerian theatre scholar and performing artist, pointed out Rotimi's "adventurous creation of a new theatre language (which) borrows from the indigenous oral tradition," using metaphor and proverbs from the Nigerian (essentially Yoruba) agrarian background; "the flora and fauna of the country—the birds, the beasts, the flowers of our native land" (Adelugba 1978, 216). To arouse tragic feelings for cathartic effect in his performances, I would argue, Akanji Nasiru advances Rotimi's deployment of "literal translation of stock Yoruba expressions and poetry"(Nasiru 1979, 23). In part consonance with these positions, I have found attitudes and concepts of Yoruba lore and culture buried in Rotimi's theatre language, especially the expression of tragic occurrences in humorous and comic moods (in the fare of slapstick comedy pointed out above). But this is done for profound philosophical appreciation through comic relief. The theatrical effect had always been to eject boredom and tedium in the dramatic fare. He had constantly employed this device to detoxify metaphysical concepts and the burdens of tragedy through simplified verbiage—what Rotimi himself has referred to as "Bad word with laughter" in *The Gods* (rendered as translated connotation of the Yoruba notion of *oro buruku on terin).*

This device also comes to capture the flavour, tones and rhythms as well as the emotional and intellectual contents of Yoruba language and thought in his 'radical' brand of English, as well-perceived in nearly all his plays, which Banham considers as a factor for the minimal critical attention to his work. This is the evocation of vernacular and pidgin languages to access both literate, semi-literate and perhaps non-literate audiences. Banham deduced that "Rotimi's work probably falls somewhat between the academic theatre of the campuses and the theatre of the popular Yoruba-language folk operas. Perhaps because of this, his work has received less critical attention than it deserves"(1988, 843). Banham has also, before me, hinted at the proposition and expound here of the growing politics of his theatre, which he describes as "an indication of Rotimi's disillusionment with the political processes in Nigeria and the increasing politicization of his dramatic art" (ibid). It is my position that his theatre language—the simplification of the linguistic medium, the essentially functional and theatrically effective deployment of oral performance elements, the use of pidgin and the polylogue through the infusion of multiple indigenous languages in his theatre, are informed by the artistic politics of his political art and theatre—for the meaning generation and message delivery purpose of dramatic art.

Without overburdening the analysis of Rotimi's theatrical form and aesthetics, we identify the proximal relationship fidelity of Rotimi's theatre mechanics and linguistic idiom with what the late Joel Adedeji established as dramaturgy total theatre—the assemblage of performance elements which comprise dance, music, gestures and spectacle– major features/characteristics of traditional Nigerian drama in his plays for aesthetic and ideological/political purposes (1971, 134-149).

The last linguistic device which I will touch on here is Rotimi's recourse to symbols. This devolves on his dramatization of the symbolic features he employs in his plays to convey meaning and make statement. This is carried out through a process of explaining the symbols dramaturgically, what I call the semiotization of his theatrical ingredients. Rotimi evokes icons, indexes and symbols for meaning-making—which is what semiotics is all about. In Yoruba, this is called *Aroko,* which is discussed remarkably and extensively by P. A. Ogundeji (1997) in his paper, 'The Communicative and Semiotic Contexts of *Aroko* among the Yoruba Symbol—Communicative Systems'. Also R. O. Ajetunmobi has, more recently, aptly referred to it as "a form of Yoruba non-verbal communication using objects and materials in varied numbers, colours of combinations with meaning" (2014). Let us just instance this from *Kurunmi.* Kurunmi, the protagonist outrightly rejects the Ogboni twins, symbolizing peace, which Alafin Adelu sent to him. In a war-mongering mood and in utter contempt for the king, Are Kurunmi sent a reply of gunpowder, symbol of war to Alafin Adelu. Kurunmi further ritualized his rejection of Adelu's symbolic offer of peace by smearing/soiling his garment with slimy okro soup. No more verbiage is needed to communicate the declaration of outright war by Kurunmi, even though words were further offered for additional dialogical impact. This is simply to illustrate the numerous instances in his plays of his deployment of symbolic gestures in theatrical contexts.

**In summary on theatre language, Rotimi surmises thus:**

a) Admitting categories and classes of audience – literate, semi and non-literate in the English language—granting them robust access into his theatre for aesthetic and didactic purposes.
b) Confirming the inevitability of the English language in his theatre and affirming the approach of "tempering its phraseology to the ear" to meet the popular audience decoding needs.
c) Attaining a close rapport with the audience.
d) Heightening his preference for performance/production in the traditional mode of open air and village, rather than the proscenium stage, Indeed, his ultimate plan, which he was very close to attaining at

Ife shortly before his death, was to build a mammoth arena stage and cast, with a robust spectacle for a communal performance, numbering thousands, whose most proximal form is the round arena setting. No use emphasizing his rejection of western stage format of the proscenium architecture.

## Conclusion

Right from the outset of his theatre career, Ola Rotimi envisioned, overtly and covertly, the struggle for identity retrieval of the subaltern (if we may tolerate that hackneyed word/concept again), minoritized majority in society through dysfunctional governance as a vocation and ideology. He has found this state of affairs to have jeopardized the viability of our nation-state which has leaned, perennially, on sub-national and ethnic loyalties. It is also responsible for the rampant state of alienation and marginalization of large sectors of our geo-polities, with a trend towards the search of selfhood at individual and group levels for alternative means of fulfilment and self-determination, away from the centre. A critical part of the options adopted is the irregular, non-formal means of dissent—the present resurgence to insurrection, multiple insurgencies by ethno-national bodies through political and sectoral violence—long anticipated in Rotimi's and other playwright's works.

Rotimi's theatre had since recognized the power of the theatre of engagement as a cultural superstructure—the power of imagination, captivation, mobilization, conscientization of theatre audience and potential real audience for social transformation. This has led him to the gravitation toward wresting and clinching a theatre language that is more amenable to the cultural and social contexts of his dramatic art, and away from Western/European norms which has for long masqueraded as universal cannons for the stage. The ultimate intervention of Rotimi's theatre is the reaffirmation and recreation of theatre as a public, communal and democratic art. He pursued this theatrical and political ideal until he breathed his last in Ile-Ife, when and where he slept and did not rise to the dawn of a new morning.

## References

Adelugba, Dapo. 1978. 'Zulu Sofola, Wale Ogunyemi, Ola Rotimi; Three Dramatists in Search of a Language' in Ogunba, O and Irele, A. (eds.) *African in Theatre*. Ibadan: University Press Ltd. 201-220.

Adedeji, Joel. 1971. 'Oral Tradition and the Contemporary Theatre in Nigeria'. *Research in African Literature*, 2.ii. 135-149.

Ajetunmobi, R.O. 2014. 'Indigenous Knowledge and Communication Systems—The Case of Yoruba Aroko.' online at Aroko-The Yoruba Hieroglyphics-Politics-Nairaland Forum.
https://www, nairaland.com>Aroko> Accessed on 06/10/22.

Banham, Martin (ed). 1988. *The Cambridge Guide to World Theatre*. Cambridge: Cambridge University Press.

Folarin, Margaret. 2002. 'Commitment to the World, Africa and Nigeria'. An Interview with Ola Rotimi in Uwatt, Effiok Bassey (ed.) *Playwriting and Directing in Nigeria: Interviews with Ola Rotimi.* Lagos (Nigeria): Apex books Ltd. 74 -78.

Nasiru, Akanji 1979. 'Ola Rotimi's Search for Technique' in Ogungbesan, Kolawole (ed.) *New West African Literature*. Heinneman: London.

Obafemi, Olu. 1996 and 2001. *Contemporary Nigerian Theatre: Cultural Heritage and Social Vision, Bayreuth*. Bayreuth African Studies and Lagos: Centre for Black and African Arts and Civilization.

Ogundeji, P.A. 1997. 'The Communication and Semiotic Contexts of Aroko among the Yoruba Symbol-Communication System'. *African Languages and Cultures*, Vol.10, No 7. 145-156.

Osofisan, F. 2016. *Insidious Treason and Beyond: Forty Years of Alternative Theatre in Nigeria*. (Essays). Ibadan. BookCraft.

# CHAPTER THREE

## The Concept of Power and Hierarchy: The Rotimian Vision of the King in *Ovonramwen Nogbaisi*

*Julie Umukoro*

### Introduction

The symbolism of African kingship is highly dependent on mystification, a portrayal of the royal self that consistently and emphatically enunciates the complex supernatural groundings of the institution of divine royal rule. To accentuate this phenomenal enigmatic self, African kings rely upon a combination of symbolic display and concealment. The efficacy of African sovereignty is therefore necessarily hinged on the esotericism of the royal personality. This chapter therefore seeks to examine the above assertions against Ola Rotimi's handling of the eponymous royal character, Oba Ovonramwen; a *Bini* king. Above all, this review of the playwright's treatment of the *Bini* (Nigeria) royalty is aimed at ascertaining the appropriateness and faithfulness of the king's imaging vis-a-vis the Bini social reality.

Nigerian monarchs are highly venerated and belong to the highest echelon of social class. Recognized as constituted authority, idolized and ranked next to the gods, Nigerian monarchs assume a sacred image. They wield power, command respect and, more often than not, engage in ritual as well as ceremonial functions of great social import in social life. Robert Brain's description of attendant functions of African royalty and, by implication, Nigeria, is worthy of attention.

Whatever the size of his realm and the extent of his power, African rulers share common themes. The chief is usually the 'owner of the land' with right to tribute; he carries out ceremonies for his people, he is often kept away from the hoi polloi; eating in private, curtained of from public or wearing a veil. His palace is set off from the people, if only by a higher hedge, and is more elaborate in design. In the palace his servants, pages and wives form a special court with special functions. (Brain 1980, 118)

To sustain the image of sacredness, an awe-inspiring figure, wealth and splendour, all elements of royal insignia, emblems, costumes, ornaments and other paraphernalia of rank, are consciously designed to accentuate the king's personality. Thus, every effort is geared toward making him a super-man of some sort. To propagate and reinforce this personality, materials that rank highest in the value chain play functional roles in royal art. Here, the use of items of inestimable value such as gold, silver, brass, ivory, coral etc. is common. Leadership symbolism in Nigeria is guided by the concepts of *superfluity*, *flamboyance* and *sumptuousness*. The preference for such symbolic elements in evoking the Nigerian leadership personality hinges on the value system that endorses such as marks of greatness. Every culture embodies a system of symbolism under which certain abstract elements assume peripheral meanings different from those naturally attributed to them. Thus, a composite notion of the collective ideas of what constitute the aesthetic basis of a typical Nigerian group is necessary for the study of its cultural symbols.

The dual concepts of *power* and *hierarchy* are fundamental to royalty in Nigerian societies, and even so much more pervasive in the '*Bini*' stereotype. The ideology on which the 'Bini' indigenous ethics is founded draws from its social, economic, religious, cultural and political institutions; all of which are inalienable binding forces of the 'Bini' royalty. The issues of power and hierarchy are prevalent in all aspects of the *Bini* royal personage, the '*Oba*' who, in all ramifications, is portrayed in the image of a demigod. This short treatise sets out to review the *Rotimian* vision of the 'Oba' (king) in *Ovonramwen Nogbaisi*, Ola Rotimi's historical play, and also seeks to establish how aptly or otherwise he has captured the concept of power and hierarchy. The *Bini* King is considered second only to the gods; indeed his image can be summed up in the words of Ola Rotimi himself, culled from an interview he granted Effiok B. Uwatt in 1985.

> Benin Royalty was, and still is a demigod. The name Ovonramwen means 'Coming from the sun'. Benin kings were themselves deities. (qtd. in Uwatt 2002, 139)

The 'master versus servant' relationship of vassal states, consolidated by the *Bini* people's prowess in war and the consequent proliferation of prisoners of war – the very foundation of slavery and hero worship – are prime factors that have created and imposed the image of supremacy on the Benin royalty. These and others have evolved into the *Bini* philosophical thoughts on social stratifications along power and hierarchical divisions and are well guided by conventions and/or practices, in furtherance of this vision. More than any African society of its era, the early Benin Empire of Nigeria, in a bid to consolidate its position as 'master' within its terrain, had ensured a more standardized and watertight power relations, and even so, a distinct hierarchical structure guided by a very severe penal and censorship system. In Benin, as in other African communal entities, identity, cultural norms, and historical specificities are consciously enunciated in cultural symbols, verbal or lyric arts, plastic arts, performance arts, body arts and other creative endeavours. All these add up to formulate the *Bini* lore and values well embedded in aphorisms, daily greetings, folktales, personal names, songs, dances, ceremonies; and also in the symbolic details of clothing, jewellery and sculpture. In effect, the *Bini* cultural objects are, in one or several other ways, signs that are reflective of basic ideas linked to their existential purpose. In fact, a *Bini* cultural artifact is an embodiment of signs, so that, it singly or collectively communicates an idea or a multiplicity of ideas; such that notions of geographical locations, professional usage, functionality, or the economic standing of the owner or user, are brought to the limelight. Reiterating this view, Firth (1936, 3) reveals that "all art is composed in a social setting" and so has a social content. The bowler hat, for instance, in addition to its functional purpose of covering the head, can at the same time be a sign of nationality, social condition, time and occasion.

More significantly, the *Bini* royal art is pervasively suffused with signs highly indexical of the kingly image as divine, sacrosanct, powerful and outstanding; so much so, his place is far removed from the human plane. This extraordinary perception of the *Bini* king is enmeshed in all of the ideas and ideals of the Benin royalty.

## About the Playwright

My main focus in this chapter, as already hinted, is on an aspect of the play, *Ovonramwen Nogbaisi*, strictly from the point of view of the playwright, which has made it quite expedient to know a little bit about the playwright himself. Emmanuel Gladstone Olawale Rotimi simply known as Ola Rotimi, the playwright of the play in focus, is one of Nigeria's multi-talented, renowned, and thorough-bred theatre idols. Besides being a playwright, Rotimi is a scholar-artist, a reputable theatre director, choreographer, actor and theatre critic. His collection of plays include: *The Gods Are Not To Blame* (1971), *Kurunmi (1972), Ovonramwen Nogbaisi* (1974), *Our Husband Has Gone Mad Again* (1977), *Holding Talks* (1979), *If...A Tragedy of the Ruled* (1983), *Hopes of the Living Dead*, (1983), *Akassa You Mi: An Historical Drama* (2001) among others. The scholarly and artistic journeys of Professor Ola Rotimi can be said to have traversed four phases.

## Phase I

Under a Nigerian Government Scholarship award in 1959 and later, as a Rockefeller Foundation scholar in play-writing, young Ola Rotimi was groomed at Boston and Yale Universities in the United States of America, from 1963 to 1966.

## Phase II

On Ola Rotimi's return to Nigeria his country, he took up a lectureship appointment in 1966 with the University of Ife (now Obafemi Awolowo University, Ile Ife) where he founded the University acting company – Ori Olokun Players – and by 1975 he was Head of the Department of Dramatic Arts of the University. During this second phase of his academic career, his fame had been well established as a director and playwright. Three of his plays which brought him to the limelight during this phase were, *The Gods Are Not To Blame* (1971), *Kurunmi* (1972) and *Ovonramwen Nogbaisi* (1974). As manuscripts, they were first staged at the Ori Olokun Cultural Centre of the University of Ife on the occasion of the annual Ife Festival of Arts in 1968, 1969, and 1971, respectively. Set against a Yoruba background, *The Gods Are Not To Blame* is an adaptation of Sophocles' *Oedipus Rex. Kurunmi* and *Ovonramwen Nogbaisi,* on the other hand, are historical dramas. Another early satirical and comic piece that also caught on like wild fire during this phase is *Our Husband Has Gone Mad Again* which takes a swipe at the political chicanery of Lejoka Brown the lead character.

## Phase III

Ola Rotimi relocated to Port Harcourt in 1977 on invitation to help plant and kick-start the Department of Creative Arts in the newly established University of Port Harcourt. The most popular of his plays credited to this phase are *Akassa You Mi* premiered in 1977 but published posthumously in 2001, *Holding Talks* (1979), *If... A Tragedy of the Ruled* (1983) and *Hopes of the Living Dead* (1988). It was also during this phase that he embarked on the writing of *Tororo Tororo Ro-Ro* and *Man Talk Woman Talk*. These were however published posthumously.

## Phase IV

After nurturing and grooming the young Department of Creative Arts, University of Port Harcourt, for more than a decade, it was time yet again for Rotimi, the erudite professor, to move on, but not without leaving a robust theatre tradition which has continued to flower at the University of Port Harcourt. He returned to the Obafemi Awolowo University in 1991. Again, the indefatigable Ola Rotimi began a professional theatre group known as the African Cradle Theatre (ACT). While still working on this, he was drawn to honour a number of invitations abroad. From 1995 to 1997 for instance, he was the Hubert H. Humphrey Visiting Professor of International Studies and Dramatic Arts and Dance at Macalister College in St Paul, Minnesota. At the end of his stay, he returned to his theatrical business at the Obafemi Awolowo University, but his activities were cut short by his sudden demise on August 18th 2000.

## About the Play

The play, *Ovonramwen Nogbaisi* derives from the historical tragedy of the eponymous hero – one of the acclaimed powerful kings of the early Benin Empire. The historical event upon which the drama draws is often referred to in history as the Benin Massacre. This is in reference to the carnage following the Benin warriors' siege against the British punitive expedition and the bloody counter response of the British, leading to the consequent restiveness, agitation and confrontations and the eventual fall and exile of the Oba. The established conflict reveals colonial officials on the one hand, determined to crush and douse the powers of the king to enable unrestricted access to free trade in the Benin territory and on the other hand, the powerful Oba (king) Ovonramwen Nogbaisi, whose grip and control of his territory created an impasse, thwarting the ambition of the British to have absolute commercial control over traders and trading in the Benin Rivers.

## About the Character *Oba* Ovonramwen

Taking a retrospective view of history, the true life Ovonramwen, regenerated in the eponymous hero of Rotimi's play, *Ovonramwen Nogbaisi,* was once a monarch of the early Benin Empire. History reveals that he reigned from 1888 to 1897. The traditional image of Benin royalty derives from a network of compatible sign images – *awe*, *sacredness*, *wealth*, *supremacy* and *grandeur*. From a holistic point of view, this network of signs is of great significance to the figure of the Oba and his office as the leader of the *Bini* race. In real life, Ovonramwen, the *Oba*, is styled with appellations that are revealing of his grandeur and power. The king is second to none, thus he is placed at the apex of the pyramid. He is, himself, seen as a god and so his domain is the sacrosanct sanctum of his people. According to a *Bini* proverb, the King is born, not made. That is to say, the *Bini* monarch is naturally enthroned or, to put it more lucidly, the throne is naturally inherited following the regulations and traditional practices of the *Bini* people. The figure of the Oba, beside his transformation and transfiguration which is duly motivated by his choice for the throne, is in turn transmogrified, so that his larger-than-life image creates the aura of awe and an ability to inspire fear in the people. This is affirmed by the power he holds over life and death. With a supernatural image the Oba is invincible, hence the does not die. At his demise, he is said to have gone to join his ancestors and as the *Bini* would put it "the chalk is broken". The following are *Bini* greetings and appellations used to eulogise the King.

## PANEGYRICS OF ỌBA OF *BINI*, SON OF Ọ̀RÀNMÍYÀN

Benin City is a reserve of rich traditions and high reverence for the traditional monarch (Oba of Benin), who once led a powerful Empire.

One of such traditions is the habit of addressing the Oba of Benin by various appellations instead of his actual names as sign of deep respect and awe. It is no wonder, therefore, that the Oba of Benin is known by several appellations.

Such appellations are:

| S/NO | BINI APPELLATION | ENGLISH TRANSLATION |
|---|---|---|
| 1 | *Ovbi' Umogun Oẓa* | The Child of the Oba whose mother hailed from Oza |
| 2 | *Ovbi' Ekpen N' Owa* | The son of the home leopard |
| 3 | Ovbi' Adimila | The son of Adimila |
| 4 | *Agbaghe, N'Ovbi Olokun* | Olokun's son, the cynosure of all mortals |
| 5 | *Abieyuwa N'Ovbi Odua N'uhe* | The son of the wealthy Odua of Uhe (Ife). |

| | | |
|---|---|---|
| 6 | *Ovbi' Ada, Ovbi' Eben* | The child of the owner of the Ada (scimitar) and Eben (royal sword), Edo symbol of sovereignty |
| 7 | *Ovbi'Ekenekene ma deyo* | The son of beauty that never fades. |
| 8 | *Ovbi'Ekuabo N'Olo, Ovbi'Ekuabo N'Olo* | The son of the rocky arm, the brave and powerful |
| 9 | *Ovbie Ikpinhianbo kpuru no Gb'oduma* | The son of the short-fingered man that was still able to kill a lion |
| 10 | Nohien utete no gh'ughe s'omwan | The king on a hill, who sees more than everybody |
| 11 | *Ovbi'Ogbonwan nei bun aro* | The son of the fearless, who looks without twinkling his eyes |
| 12 | *Ovbi'ode, ode n'ohan ren mu' ete* | The son of the warrior whose enemies got frightened at the announcement of the approach |
| 13 | *Uku Akpolokpolo* | The mighty that rules |
| 14 | *Ovbi' Adolo no dolo uwa dolo utomwen* | The son of the wise judge and peacemaker who combined wisdom and wealth with long life. |
| 15 | *Ovbi' oven owie no gbaisi* | The son of the morning sun that covers everywhere |
| 16 | *Ovbi' Akpogunla, ogie no y'igho b'owa* | The child of the womb of Akpogunla – the warrior who fought big wars and built a house of cowries |
| 17 | *Oba n'osa* | A King that is god |
| 18 | *Ovbi' otolo n'olomi; Ologberonmwon nei rie iruen, ebo, ayemwinre eminiminimini* | The son of the water controller, the son of beauty itself, the starter of things and the person whose reign saw people with many tongues |

These appellations are in cognizance of the greatness of the Omo n'oba ne edo, the Oba of Benin.

*Oba gha tor kpere!/* Long Live the King!

Iseee (Source: Adulawo TV Feb 25, 2020)

## The Concept of Power and Hierarchy

Ola Rotimi, in his play, *Oba Ovonramwen* (1974), has consciously and appropriately given concern to the depiction of the Oba to tally with the image of supremacy ceded him in social reality. To evoke this, Rotimi conveys the ideas of the king's awesomeness in his choice of words to describe his person or throne. He uses such appellations as *'Your Greatness', 'Your Highness', 'Your Majesty' 'Great one' 'Our Lord'* and so on. Imageries, metaphors and symbols are constantly explored by Rotimi to delineate the nature and the subliminal ethos of the king's image. Again, Rotimi resorts to the use of animal imagery to connote the King's might relative to his economic, political, martial, spiritual and mystic strength. Thus the Oba's strength is envisioned in the image of such powerful animals as the leopard, lion, tiger etc. Rotimi refers to him as "the home leopard" (Rotimi, 4) *Ovbi' Ekpen N' Owa (*see no 2 in the table of appellations above). Again, Ola Rotimi compares the King's bulk to that of an elephant (7) and describes him as the moon compared to the chiefs who are described as tiny little stars (9). Still using the imagery of the moon, the quote below is apt.

> Some men there are who think that by honour of years, or the power of position, or by too much love for trouble, they can dull the fullness of my glow and bring darkness to the empire…Henceforth a full moon's, my glow… dominant andunopen to rivalry throughout the empire. (Rotimi, 7)

The Oba's wealth, grandeur and mystical self are established through vivid and informative dialogue and stage directions. Ola Rotimi in his opening stage directions speaks of "the imposing figure of the Oba" (4) who "with slow dignity…strides unrushed" (4). The pictorial image evoked here is one that dwarfs or diminishes whatever else beside him. On the issue of the Oba's supremacy and the general attitude of the *Bini* people toward him, Ahmed Yerima, another Nigerian playwright who has also written a historical play on Oba Ovonramwen, titled *The Trials of Oba Ovonramwen* (1998), and drawing from the same historical source, also corroborates the views on the supremacy of the King and his position of power in his domain. Speaking through his characters, namely Burrows asserts that the Oba stands as a "Symbol of life and death" to his people (Yerima, 58). Obaseki hails him "Ovonramwen no'gie, my life (ibid, 33). Carter says "the Oba's power is supreme" (ibid, 59). Ologbose, on the other hand, confirms the *Oba's* authority, saying "the Oba commands and we obey" (ibid, 38). The *Oba*, as the stage directions reveal, by merely raising his hands, orders total tranquillity among the chiefs (ibid, 37). The royal flesh is so sacred that rather than allow either "arrows" or the "Whiteman's bullet" to desecrate it in war, a warrior chief must fence such missiles off with his own chest (ibid, 24).

At this juncture, it is pertinent to take a deeper look into this concept of the *Oba's* supremacy. What is it that imposes this image of power on the king? How is it that in hierarchy he is considered next to the gods or considered and worshiped as a god? (See table of appellation nos. 4 & 17 above) *Agbaghe, N'Ovbi Olokun* (Olokun's son, the cynosure of all mortals). *Oba n'osa* (A King that is a god). Appellation 4 names the *Oba*, son of Olokun, the sea god. Indeed, he is often referred to as the terrestrial counterpart of Olokun. This ascribes to him the god image. The symbol of the *Oba's* power is his royal regalia made up of the *erhu ede* (royal crown), *ugbudian ivie* (beaded fly whisk), *ewu-ivie n'ovien iye* (beaded top dress), *odigba* (beaded collar), *ada* (scimitar) and *eben* (royal sword), *Bini* symbol of sovereignty.

The *Bini* royal regalia, like any other Nigerian stereotype, is designed with a conscious effort to propagate the larger-than-life image imposed on the *Oba*. The King's robe or loin-cloth as the case may be is often larger in proportion than the everyday wear of commoners. Censored royal prestige items such as the aforementioned are also most efficacious in symbolizing the image of the *Bini* king. With the sole intention to transform and heighten the impact of the King's personality, the royal ensemble, take on a quasi-magical aura, assuming metonymical images. It symbolizes his divinity, economic power, status or station, among other things. The long-bladed *ada* and *eben* as traditional emblems of authority symbolize the right of the Oba to take human life. Although certain grades of chiefs are allowed the privilege of the use of *ada* and *eben* as paraphernalia of their offices, they are to be used as mere insignia. In comparison, the King's *ada* and *eben* are more superior in quality, bigger in size and with more embellishment. Other notable paraphernalia of the *Oba* are animal artifacts such as horns, teeth, skin, skulls etc. Also prevalent are bronze and brass sculptures, steel and carved models of ancient war implements. Colour symbolism has also been widely explored in the assemblage of the *Bini* royal image.

There is a predominant and recurrent use of white and red. 'White', which generally carries the aura of 'cleanliness' and 'transparency' in *Bini* cosmology, is used to evoke concepts of 'innocence', 'holiness', 'incorruptibility' and 'virtuousness'. White is, therefore, seen as a positive element associated with the joyous or happy occasion. Red, on the other hand, retains the connotation of danger in *Bini* land: hence, it is significantly used to symbolize war costumes. Regardless of aesthetics, the recurrence of the 'white' and 'red' colour combination in the *Bini* costume of royalty is symbolic. Drawn upon their presumed connotation of 'life' and 'death' respectively, 'white' and 'red' visibly enunciate the notion of the king as one who wields power over life and death. Just as the king can order the death of an offending party, so does he reserve the right to retract a death sentence when he deems fit. From the above discussions, it is quite obvious that it the royal regalia that imposes this image of power on the *Oba*. By its nature, it assumes significance as a ritual ensemble with the aura of sacredness and potent power. After the approved rites of coronation and investiture, the would-be *Oba* is dressed up, in his royal regalia, comprising all the paraphernalia of his office, with the crown coming last. The moment his head bears the crown and the king makers hail him with the symbolic greeting of "*Oba gha tor kpere*!" (Long Live the King!), he becomes completely transmogrified. The act transforms his humanity; so that he becomes a potent supernatural force with power over the lives of his subjects. Ahmed Yerima, also portends the significance of the crown to the Bini people in his play, *The Trials of Oba Ovonramwen,* when he refers to it as "the soul of the Bini people" (Yerima, 70) and therefore worth guarding even at the peril of one's life. In reference to his position, stature and power, he is associated with the sun or the moon, so far removed and out of human reach. The name Ovonramwen means "Coming from the sun". His commands are obeyed without question. He would only need to utter the words for action to commence. This is illustrated in the play when the Oba orders the deaths of Obaruduagbon and Esasoyen and the immediate response of the drums, "the Oba's will be done" (Rotimi, 6). The Benin Culture "places the Oba at a pedestal above ordinary beings. A pedestal akin to that reserved for the gods" (Uwatt, 2002, 139).

In conclusion, Ola Rotimi has successfully and appropriately written a historical drama on the Bini kingdom which has faithfully documented the image of Oba Ovonramwen and, by extension, the image of every Oba of Benin. Considering the exhaustive treatment of cultural issues in the play it is a significant documentation for posterity, historians, researchers, scholars of theatre and cultural enthusiasts working on the Bini royal personage. This documentation will also serve as a blueprint and guide for the theatrical practitioner who is desirous of producing a play on the *Bini* royalty.

## References

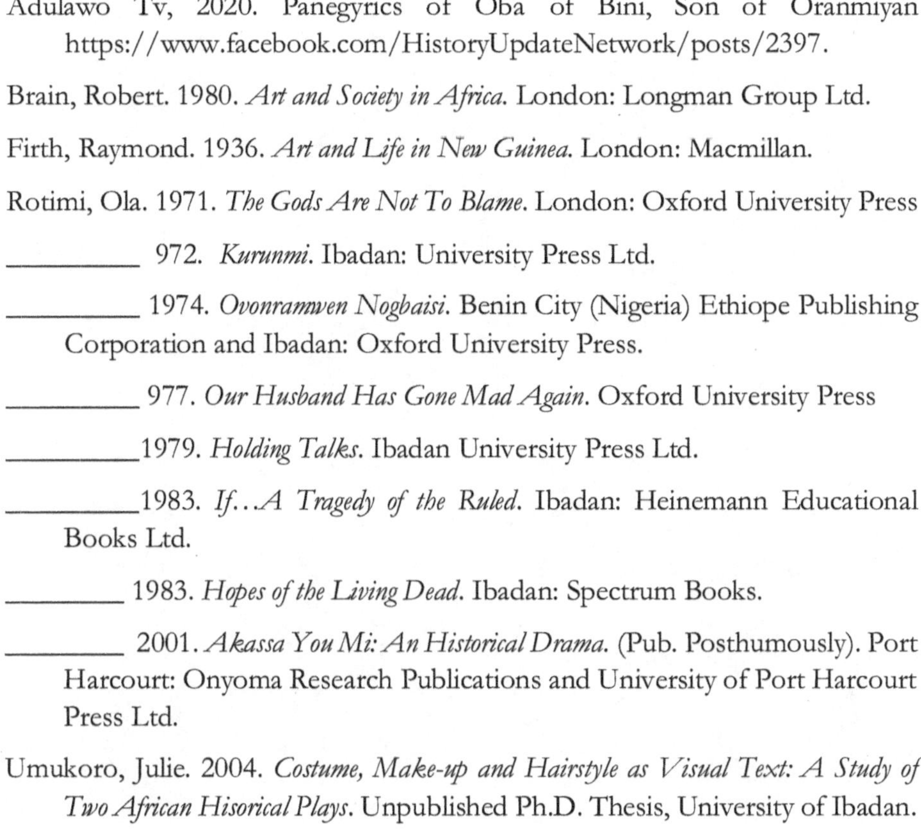

Adulawo Tv, 2020. Panegyrics of Oba of Bini, Son of Oranmiyan https://www.facebook.com/HistoryUpdateNetwork/posts/2397.

Brain, Robert. 1980. *Art and Society in Africa.* London: Longman Group Ltd.

Firth, Raymond. 1936. *Art and Life in New Guinea.* London: Macmillan.

Rotimi, Ola. 1971. *The Gods Are Not To Blame.* London: Oxford University Press

__________ 972. *Kurunmi.* Ibadan: University Press Ltd.

__________ 1974. *Ovonramwen Nogbaisi.* Benin City (Nigeria) Ethiope Publishing Corporation and Ibadan: Oxford University Press.

__________ 977. *Our Husband Has Gone Mad Again.* Oxford University Press

__________1979. *Holding Talks.* Ibadan University Press Ltd.

__________1983. *If…A Tragedy of the Ruled.* Ibadan: Heinemann Educational Books Ltd.

_________ 1983. *Hopes of the Living Dead.* Ibadan: Spectrum Books.

_________ 2001. *Akassa You Mi: An Historical Drama.* (Pub. Posthumously). Port Harcourt: Onyoma Research Publications and University of Port Harcourt Press Ltd.

Umukoro, Julie. 2004. *Costume, Make-up and Hairstyle as Visual Text: A Study of Two African Hisorical Plays.* Unpublished Ph.D. Thesis, University of Ibadan.

Uwatt, Effiok Bassey (ed.). 2002.*Playwriting and Directing in Nigeria: Interviews with Ola Rotimi* Lagos (Nigeria): Apex books Ltd.

Yerima, Ahmed. 1998. *The Trials of Oba Ovonramwen.* Ibadan (Nigeria) Kraftbooks Ltd.

# CHAPTER FOUR

## Ola Rotimi: The Best National Troupe's Artistic Director Nigeria Never Had

*Duro Oni*

### Introduction

Writing a tribute has never been an easy task, especially with the scepticism that attends to most tributes. The general reception has always been that the one writing the tribute cannot but eulogize his/her subject to high heavens. What else would one who decides to write a tribute do than to praise the subject of his treatise appears to be the refrain on the lips of many sceptics. As Olu Obafemi points out, "there are those who will never believe that one can write objectively about close friends, without lapsing into uncritical eulogies or sheer panegyrics" (2012, 696). Yet, as William James perceptibly points out, "When we die, it is as if an eye of the world were closed. Perceptions from the eye may cease, but the memories and conceptual relations that have spun themselves round the perceptions of that person remains in the larger earth-life as distinct as ever" (qtd. in Walls 2020, 14). This is very true of Ola Rotimi, notwithstanding that his play texts have not received the critical attention they deserve (Banham 1998, 843). Although it has been more than 22 years now that he passed on to eternal glory, his legacy still lives on; it still "remains in the larger earth-life as distinct as ever."

This fact more than any whimsical desire to write a tribute has informed this chapter contribution in which I examine Ola Rotimi's private life as well as his influence and impact as a playwright and director in the Nigerian theatrical practice against the backdrop of the search at a time for an Artistic Director for the National Troupe of Nigeria (NTN) in which I was an active participant. The chapter interrogates the potential list of candidates who were to be considered for the position; their background training and their experience as directors to take over from Hubert Ogunde who was engaged by the Federal Government of Nigeria to help assemble and select the first set of the members of what was to become the National Troupe of Nigeria (NTN). While not invalidating or discountenancing the various contributions that other Artistic Directors after

Hubert Ogunde have made to the development of the NTN, it is nonetheless because of my firm conviction of what could have been had Ola Rotimi been appointed as Artistic Director, and had he accepted, that has birthed this chapter contribution. Noteworthy is the fact that the alternative title that I elected for this chapter contribution is 'Remembering Ola Rotimi, A Complete Man of the Theatre, 20 Years On.' Having served as playwright, director, head of department of creative arts at the University of Port-Harcourt, lecturer at University of Ife (now Obafemi Awolowo University) as well as visiting professor and director in Germany and Italy, as well as at DePauw University, Greencastle, Indiana and Wabash College, Crawfordsville, Indiana, the assertion that Ola Rotimi is the best Artistic Director that the National Troupe of Nigeria (NTN) never had is not mere speculation. The assertion is not predicated on just satisfying the requirements of paying glowing tribute to a dead friend. Rather, it is predicated primarily on his contribution to theatrical practice in Nigeria.

This contribution is not only as a playwright and critic, but also as a director, producer, and innovator and manager of a theatre space and company. Ola Rotimi was an actor, director, choreographer and designer – who created performance spaces, influenced by traditional architectural forms (Martin Banham, 2000). Accordingly, as with the case with most first-generation Nigerian dramatists, he bridged the gap between drama as text and drama as theatre. He wrote and staged his own plays, which he used to speak to political powers, thereby speaking for the oppressed masses, and becoming the conscience of his society.

Martin Banham acknowledges the talents of Ola Rotimi as a writer and director (1998, 843). Following on the heels of Banham, Chinyere G. Okafor also observes that "[t]he contribution of Ola Rotimi to the development of drama in Nigeria has been significant. His achievement and input is not only as a playwright and critic but also as a director and producer" (1990, 24). Based on these contributions to the Nigerian theatre practice, he has been variously described by critics. Sanya Osha describes him as a "fastidious teacher, taskmaster, and theatre visionary" (*Brittle Paper* 2022), while Sunday Joseph Ayodabo's description is that he is "one of the most outstanding Nigerian playwrights, an accomplished theatre director and consummate aesthete" (2016, 72). For Chinyere Okafor, she glowingly described him as "a giant in the Nigerian stage world" and as "a renowned man of the theatre" (1990, 29).

## The Search for an Artistic Director

Not surprisingly, upon the death in 1990 of Hubert Ogunde, who had been invited in 1986 as a consultant to set up and serve as the first Artistic Director of the National Troupe of Nigeria, Prof Ola Rotimi's name ranked highest among those being considered as a possible replacement. As at this period, quite a number of theatre stage directors that were popular and famous resided in the university system. These included Dapo Adelugba, Bayo Oduneye and Demas Nwoko (all at the University of Ibadan); Ola Rotimi (University of Ife); and Uriel Worika (Rivers State Arts Council). While Dapo Adelugba had directed *Langbodo* by Wale Ogunyemi as the FESTAC Drama entry for Nigeria, Demas Nwoko choreographed the dance entry of *Children of Paradise*. Ola Rotimi, on his part had a string of successful productions with *The Gods are not to Blame* and *Kurunmi*, while Uriel Worika also had a successful run of Elechi Amadi's *Isiburu* at the National Theatre Main Hall (originally called Main Bowl).

At his exit, any of these stage directors could have easily slipped into Hubert Ogunde's moccasins to pilot the stagecraft of the NTN. But as the Special Assistant/Adviser to the Honourable Minister of Culture from 1990 - 1991, some others and I had embarked on developing a *modus operandi* for the National Theatre and National troupe of Nigeria and the prospective Chief Executives and supporting staff, after Hubert Ogunde's pioneering work at raising and managing the Troupe. As already indicated, Prof Ola Rotimi's name ranked the highest among those being considered. His name echoed within and through the panelled walls of our meeting places. Unfortunately, certain changes occurred in Ministerial postings and the then Minister of Culture was deployed to the Ministry of Youth and Sports, and a new Minister was deployed from the Ministry of Transport. By the time that the appointments were later to be made in 1991, a lot of water had run under the bridge. As the cliché goes, the rest is now history.

## The Objectives of the National Troupe of Nigeria

The consideration of Ola Rotimi, and his almost eventual appointment as the Artistic Director of the NTN was against the backdrop of the stated objectives of NTN, which, as would be seen shortly, appears to be objectives designed and formulated with Ola Rotimi in mind. As outlined in the law (Decree No. 47 of 1991), the objectives of the Board of the NTN, among others, shall be to:

a) encourage the discovery and development of talents in the performing arts;
b) achieve high artistic productions specifically designed for national and international tours;
c) ensure that productions of the Troupe are geared towards national aspirations;
d) encourage the development of children's theatre; and
e) ensure the preservation of the repertoire of the Troupe.

In all these aspects, as we considered them then, Ola Rotimi's name kept jumping on us and reoccurring in our deliberations. Thus, as controversial as the title of this chapter contribution might be, it emanates from what actually happened during the search for an Artistic Director, which as I have stated, I was an active participant.

## Ola Rotimi Himself

Unless a prophet is called and anointed, s/he cannot lay claim to such an exalted office. Ola Rotimi from the cradle appears to be an anointed prophet of stage craft. He appears to have been destined from the cradle to become the giant of Nigerian theatre, and a renowned man of the theatre. George Bernard Shaw in his glowing remarks about Lady Augusta Gregory who wrote plays for the stage in Ireland might as well have been writing about Ola Rotimi when he stated that:

> If ever there was a person doomed from the cradle to write for the stage, to break through every social obstacle to get to the stage, to refuse to do anything but write for the stage, nay, to invent and create a theatre if no theatre existed, that person is… (qtd. in Remport 2018, 1)

The missing item in the ellipsis above is the name Lady Augusta Gregory. Yet, the name can conveniently be replaced with that of Ola Rotimi as the remarks also hold very true for him as can be seen from the very remarkable background into which he was born.

Olawale Gladstone Emmanuel Rotimi, best known as Ola Rotimi was born on the 13th of April, 1938, as the youngest of three children, in Sapele in the present-day Delta State to Samuel Gladstone Enitan Rotimi a Yoruba steam-launch engineer (a successful director and an amateur producer of plays) and Dorcas Adolae Oruene Addo an Ijaw drama enthusiast, who herself managed a dance troupe. Owing to the orientation of his parents, Rotimi even first appeared on stage at the age 4 in a play directed and produced by his father, an amateur theatre practitioner (Coker Jr. 1992, 60). What is remarkable about the parentage of Ola Rotimi is not just that they are drama and theatre enthusiasts, but also the multi-ethnic background their marriage afforded Rotimi. This multi-ethnic and theatre family into which Ola Rotimi was born was undoubtedly very influential on his dramaturgy. Having been introduced at an early age to acting on stage, it is not surprising that Rotimi would grow to love drama and the theatre as well as become one of the leading Nigerian theatre artists. Moreover, in a country like Nigeria that is torn apart by ethnic cleavages and tribalism, the multi-ethnic background of Rotimi becomes a rare advantage. Rotimi "speaks English, Yoruba, Ijaw, Igbo, Hausa, and pidgin and a few other Nigerian tongues" (Okafor 1990, 25). With such a background, it is not a surprise that his name would rank highest as part of his job responsibilities as the Artistic Director of the NTN would have been to work with members of the troupe who have been recruited from various ethnic nationalities of the Nigerian nation-state. The thinking then, which still holds true presently, is that he would be in a position to interact easily with the members of the troupe as well as bring out the best in them since he understands their various cultural backgrounds and orientations.

Although not so much a consideration, also significant was the training and education that Ola Rotimi received. He was one of the first trained Theatre Artistes in Nigeria. On a scholarship from the Nigerian government in 1959, Rotimi studied theatre at Boston University and from 1963 to 1966 he earned a Master of Fine Arts degree in playwriting and dramatic literature at Yale University on a Rockefeller Foundation Fellowship. Whereas Okafor validly remarks that Rotimi's formal training and education in the USA "equipped him with knowledge of the arts of the theatre as well as critical ability and exposed him to the world of literature and the arts in general" and that "[a]ll this training and exposure later yielded artistic fruit in his numerous plays and productions" (1990, 24), what is also certain is that it is on the strength of this foreign exposure and training that Ola Rotimi formulated his dramatic arts in opposition to western ideals. Omotayo Oloruntoba-Oju argues that the contributions of Ola Rotimi and Wole Soyinka within the context of multiculturalism, "lies in the fact that their drama highlights the conflict inherent in the cohabitation of cultures, more so in situations where the indigenous cultural perspectives are threatened by the hegemonic inclinations of invading cultures" (2014, 76–77). He then adds that "their *modus operandi* is the theatrical juxtaposition of the indigenous way of life with contending cultures and the deployment of characters, dialogue and spectacle on either side of the contending arguments" (ibid, 78). While studying abroad is not necessarily an essential criterion for African writers to affirm their indigenous culture, experiencing first-hand the hegemonic and supercilious disposition of the western world appears to pronounce the intensity of such a need, and make it more poignant. Ola Rotimi can, therefore, be said to be like the poet persona of Wole Soyinka's 'Telephone Conversation' or like Olunde in Soyinka's *Death and the King's Horseman* – both of whom affirm their person and their culture in the face of the pernicious denigration of Eurocentric ideology that they experience first-hand. On the foregoing note, it can be argued that Ola Rotimi would have ensured that the productions of the NTN are geared towards national aspirations.

The marriage of Ola Rotimi was also of significance in terms of the direction that his theatrical practice took. In 1965, he married Hazel Mae Gaudreau, a French-Canadian, who also studied at Boston University, where she majored in opera, voice and music education. Married to a French-Canadian, and having spent much of the 1990s, owing in part to the political conditions in Nigeria, living in the Caribbean and the United States, where he taught at Macalaster College in St. Paul, Minnesota (*Encyclopaedia Britannica*), Rotimi can be said to be a citizen of the world. Moreover, as a music expert, Hazel undoubtedly contributed to her husband's theatre productions, especially in the area of music and dance. Although Martin Banham submits that "[t]he popularity of" Rotimi's theatre "in the late 1960s and early 1970s was the result not only of the talents of Rotimi as a writer and director, but also of the considerable musical talents of the composer Akin Euba" (1998, 843), there is no doubt that Ola Rotimi would have also benefitted from the musical expertise of his wife. Okafor even argues that it is with the help of his musician wife that Rotimi "directs the music and choreographs the dance" of his plays (1990, 25). In this context, Ola Rotimi must have been alluding to the influence of his wife on his theatricality when he acknowledged the crucial influence of music to his dramaturgy. He admits that, "Without music, I can't even get the inspiration to write a play, let alone stage one. I'm inspired by music and I articulate my dramatic formulations through music" (Okafor 1990, 25).

## Ola Rotimi's Theatre

This total theatre of Ola Rotimi in which drumming, music, and dance are important aspects of the entire sequence of his stage productions was also apposite in his consideration as the possible replacement for Hubert Ogunde. Omotayo Oloruntoba-Oju observes that in the plays of first-generation dramatists, which includes Ola Rotimi, theatre was 'total'. In his words, they do "not deploy spectacle only as an incident or occasional theatrical or carnival event within the sequence; rather, the various elements of indigenous theatre, including drums, dance and the deployment of indigenous dialogic codes, suffuse the entire sequences that make up a play or a production" (80). It is common knowledge that "As a playwright, Rotimi weaves music into the structure of (his) plays" and "As a producer, he directs the music and choreographs the dance" of his plays (Okafor 1990, 25). From 1971 to 2000, I was fortunate to have watched a number of productions of Ola Rotimi in several venues in Nigeria, where I witnessed all these first hand. They include: *The Gods Are Not to Blame*; *Kurunmi*; Ovonramwen Nogbaisi; *Our Husband Has Gone Mad Again*; *Holding Talks*; *Grip Am*; *If: A Tragedy of the Ruled;* and *Hopes of the Living Dead*. What is remarkable about all these productions is that, reminiscent of Derek Bullock of the old Government College, Ibadan, Ola Rotimi's directorial style included detailed characterization. All his characters had a specific action to perform. There really was "Never a dull moment"! He was particularly adept in arranging and choreographing crowd scenes which were expertly handled. His blocking and expert blending of drama, music and dance were his forte. To many, then, this style of drama gave Rotimi an edge since the NTN was not only about drama, but also about music and dance.

Writing about Ola Rotimi's theatre would not be complete without highlighting his creation and establishment of the Ori Olokun Courtyard. This was very remarkable since what his formal education and training in America introduced him to was the proscenium and amphitheatre kind of stage. But with the firm conviction that these forms were foreign impositions on Nigerian dramatic arts, Ola Rotimi transcended the boundaries of western theatre as well as his training and education to create and establish the Ori Olokun Courtyard, which is a theatre that could not strictly be described in the round, but more of a three-sided audience sitting area. This was adequately captured by Banham when he explains that:

> There, the Ori Olokun acting company performed in an arts centre that Rotimi and his colleagues converted out of a disused hotel. Its open courtyard was altered to admit audiences on three sides, breaking any imported sense of a proscenium arch and allowing for a dramaturgy that utilised Nigerian performance forms, where audience and actors interact in the same space. (Banham, 2000)

In previous studies on Performance Venues in Nigeria, I have established that the Courtyard Theatres were the most effective for Nigerian plays (see Oni 1985).

Such outdoor theatres include those at the University of Jos and the Ahmadu Bello University Studio Theatre (developed by Mike Etherton and Andrew Horn with architects and designers from the university). Hence, the Ori Olokun Courtyard Theatre which Ola Rotimi established, and where he operated was considered a phenomenon. As has been noted, "[t]he Ori Olokun experiment was a remarkable attempt to design a modern stage loyal to an authentically traditional situation" (Okafor 1990, 29). Rotimi himself argued that "[m]odern theatre in Nigeria must have allegiance to its traditional source. We cannot change modern times, but we must have appendages of our past to our present in order to qualify our entitlements to Africanity" (Coker Jr. 1992, 62). Therefore, even in the aspect of his establishment of the Ori Olokun Courtyard, Ola Rotimi once more demonstrated that his theatre is fundamentally geared towards national aspirations.

Ola Rotimi used this traditional Ori Olokun setting in seamless scene changes for effective dramatization. My very first encounter and amazing experience of the ambience of the Ori Olokun Courtyard was in 1971 during the production of *The Gods Are Not To Blame*, adapted from *Oedipus Rex* with Femi Robinson/Kola Oyewo as King Odewale and Cleopatra Okonye as Queen Ojuola. The performances were powerful renditions of productions in a traditional courtyard theatre. Other productions watched later were Ola Rotimi's *Kurunmi* with Akin Sofoluwe as lead actor. A year after, Ola Rotimi staged his classic production of *Ovonramwen Nogbaisi* at the Institute of African Studies Courtyard at the University of Ibadan (UI) with Jimi Solanke as lead actor. Other actors included Segun Marcus, who later served as a Permanent Secretary in the Lagos State Government. A few of the white lecturers at Ife joined in the production which contrasted with Dapo Adelugba's production of *Kiriji* by Wale Ogunyemi in which the white characters in the play were played by black actors who were whitened up as a parody of the white skin. Other performances that were also staged at the Ori Olokun Courtyard, apart from those written and directed by Ola Rotimi, which were nonetheless amazing and were unforgettable experiences of watching plays in a traditional theatre included productions in the different genres of Dance and Musical Productions. These included Peggy Harper's *Alatangana* and *Purapakali* and Akin Euba's *Chaka*. Some of these were also produced for and at the Ife Festival of Arts and Culture with such great actors and dancers like Peter Badejo, Bose Ayeni (later Tsevende), Peter Fatomilola and Tunji Ojeyemi.

## Ola Rotimi's Apprenticeship Theatre

In addition to Ola Rotimi's theatre in itself, therefore, another factor that swayed the consideration for an Artistic Director in his favour is the kind of apprenticeship theatre he operated, which was in line with the first objective of NTN to encourage the discovery and development of talents in the performing arts. Adeniyi Coker Jr. notes that "the performers at Ori Olokun were a rare group, made up of students, farmers, labourers, academicians (sic), mechanics and so on. It included both the educated and people with little achievement in terms of western education…" (1992, 70). For instance, his four children were active participants in his dramatic productions. Moreover, some of the most famous actors in Nigeria at that time emanated from his stable. They included Femi Robinson/Kola Oyewo (King Odewale in *The Gods*, Cleopatra Okonye as Queen Ojuola); Akin Sofoluwe (Kurunmi); Jimi Solanke (Ovonranwen Nogbaisi); Gboyega Ajayi in *Grip Am*; Ola Rotimi Himself in *Holding Talks;* and Columbus Irisonga as Harcourt Whyte in *Hopes of the Living Dead.* What was outstanding about Ola Rotimi is that he worked with actors that were fluent in English and others that were hardly literate, but he used them effectively and they played their roles well. His philosophical disposition appeared to favour a style of directing and coaching of actors; some kind of apprenticeship system even though he drove his cast and himself hard! He was a taskmaster per excellence. Yet, he elevated and transformed the minds of those he worked with, whether educated or not. This, and the fact that his plays draw from the historical realities of the Nigerian nation-state, undoubtedly, also provided him with another edge as the possible Artistic Director of the National Troupe of Nigeria.

## Conclusion

Did Ola Rotimi desire to be the Artistic Director of the National Theatre/Troupe of Nigeria? If he had been appointed, would he have accepted? It has been speculated, given the independence of mind that Ola Rotimi had, that even if offered the appointment, would he have accepted it? These are Questions we may never get Answers to! However, when Ola Rotimi passed on in the year 2000, my senior colleague (Prof Emeritus Femi Osofisan) and I led the Ministerial delegation to his funeral in Ile Ife and I had the privilege of reading the funeral oration at the Oduduwa outdoor theatre; and below were my parting shots from some of the popular proverbs of Ola Rotimi, culled from *The Gods Are Not To Blame*:

*Is it not ignorance that makes the rat attack the cat?*

*The hyena flirts with the hen, the hen is happy, not knowing that her death has come.*

*The mangrove tree dwells in the river, but does that make it a crocodile?*

*Can the cockroach be innocent in a gathering of fowls?*

*The toad likes water, but not when the water is boiling.*

## Long Live the King

The Theatre Directing King of Nigeria is Dead … more than twenty-two years after, long live the King, Prof Olawale Gladstone Emmanuel Rotimi (1938-2000); may God keep and protect his children Enitan Rotimi and Kole-Hayward Rotimi. Ola Rotimi's dream was to direct a performance that would involve 5000 cast members (see https://dawncommission.org). Rotimi's aspiration perhaps came to pass after his death when he was being laid to rest at the Amphi Africa Theatre shortly before his internment, thousands of mourners filed past his casket, which was placed on a stage, to perform their individual roles of paying their last respect to the fallen theatre icon. It was indeed a grand event and a spectacularly dramatic farewell to the best national troupe's director Nigeria never had.

## References

Ayodabo, Sunday Joseph. 2016. 'Traditionalism as a Source of Change: Ola Rotimi's *Kurunmi* as an Epitome' in *Venets: The Belogradchik Journal for Local History, Cultural Heritage and Folk Studies,* 7. 1 (2016). 68 – 89.

Banham, Martin. 1998. *The Cambridge Guide to World Theatre.* Cambridge University Press.

Banham, Martin. 2000. 'Ola Rotimi: Playwright who put Nigeria's dramas on the stage.' *The Guardian*, October 20th, 2000. (Retrieved on 2nd October 2022).

Coker, Adeniyi Jr. 1992. 'The Contest and Development of Ola Rotimi at the Ori Olokun Theater' in *Journal of Black Studies,* 23. 1 (Sep. 1992). 60 – 74.

*Encyclopaedia Britannica.* (https://www.britannica.com)

Obafemi, Olu. 2012. 'Duro Oni at Sixty: Light Out of the Dark' in Sunday Enessi Ododo (ed.) *Fireworks for a Lighting Aesthetician: Essays and Tributes in Honour of Duro Oni @ 60.* 696 – 698.

Okafor, Chinyere G. 1990. 'Ola Rotimi: The Man, the Playwright, and the Producer on the Nigerian Theater Scene' in *World Literature Today,* 64. 1 (Winter 1990). 24 – 29.

Oloruntoba-Oju, Omotayo. 2014. 'Theatre of the Rooted and Theatre of the Uprooted: Comparing Multiculturalism in African and Caribbean Theatre' in *Caribbean Quarterly,* 60. 3 (September 2014). 73 – 88.

Oni, Duro. 1985. 'Plays and Presentation Mode in Nigeria: A Technical Outlook' in *Nigerian Theatre Journal,* 2. 1 & 2. (1985). 198 - 205.

Osha, Sanya. 2022. 'Ori Olokun: Remembering the Dramaturgy of Ola Rotimi' in *Brittle Paper,* April 19th, 2022.

Remport, Eglantina. 2018. *Bernard Shaw and His Contemporaries: Lady Gregory and Irish National Theatre, Art, Drama, Politics.* Switzerland: Palgrave Macmillan.

Walls, Laura Dassow. 2004. 'The Fire Within: A Tribute to Bob Richardson' in *The Thoreau Society Bulletin,* 311. (Fall 2020). 14 – 15.

# Part II

# Tributes to and Reminisces on Ola Rotimi

# CHAPTER FIVE

## Professor Olawale Rotimi (Himself): 'The Theatre Wizard'

*Peter Badejo*

It is doubtful if enough has been written, discussed or recognized in reference to the performance arts and artists who contributed to the Ori Olokun Experimental Workshop Project. Whenever Ori Olokun is mentioned in documentations or presentation at conferences, the references are usually to the visual arts. Other art forms in the workshop seem to be relegated to the sidelines or forgotten all together. However, both visual and performance art forms were all explored at the Ori Olokun 1968 workshop. Print making, sculpture, batik, painting, drama, dance, music, singing and acting were all subjects from the beginning, and these were influential for what became the Visual and Dramatic Arts School of the University of Ife. The insufficient reference in documentations and debates on the performance aspects of Ori Olokun experiment could be attributed to the dearth of scholars who are interested in documenting this aspect of the workshop and its contributions. This tribute, therefore, to Professor Olawale Rotimi, one of the sole contributors to the success of Ori Olokun, may throw light on these missing links.

Let me start by looking at three important factors in the development and influence of Rotimi on Ori Olokun and the development of theatre, which hopefully will highlight the above issue. First, the emergence of the University of Ife gave birth to the Institute of African Studies which became the Centre for Research and Development in African art and culture. Secondly, the role of many notable artists, researchers, and professionals who joined the University of Ife to develop the research and arts endeavor. Third, the critically important role played by Ola Rotimi, one of Ori Olokun's key researchers, in creating and developing a disciplined program to train performing artists.

### The Source: University of Ife (1961)

The Yoruba people are known for their curiosity as seekers of knowledge, learning and development. The University of Ife was therefore seen as a laudable enterprise for the Yoruba people by virtue of the fact that it was an off-spring of the University of Ibadan, the Nigerian premier institution of higher learning. Ife University was conceptualized and based in Ibadan where it was nurtured under the premiere institution until its home-coming to its permanent site in Ife in 1967. Through the incredible vision of the founding fathers of University of Ife, under its second Vice Chancellor Hezekiah Oluwasanmi (1966–75), well-thought-out plans were tirelessly worked out, developed and executed with ease. Academic faculties grew with newly structured facilities, buildings that were appropriately equipped, hostels for students, lecture rooms etc., all sprang up, and these helped to entice and captivate external attention. Thanks to the conducive environment created by the political system at the time that sincerely appreciated and valued education. The university attracted brilliant academicians (lecturers and researchers), knowledgeable administrators, nationally and internationally, who came to join the progressive institution with pleasure.

In Ile-Ife, the tertiary institution exhibited traits of greatness early on with focus and purpose in developing faculties and departments of repute. Living true to its foundational concept "Ife for Learning and Culture", it began to rank among higher institutions of note both in quality of studies and growth of academic excellence. As a result, the University of Ife rapidly became internationally recognized. Even so, it was a roller-coaster of development.

One such successful development was, and continues to be, the Institute of African Studies. IAS was under the tutelage of an experienced director Mr. Michael Crowder, a Briton (Professor of History), who had worked at the University of Ibadan's Institute of African Studies. Ife Institute attracted dynamic and able researchers who contributed towards its building. Among them were Dr Solomon Irinie Wangboje, PhD in Arts Education with specialization in print-making and textile design; Mr. P.R.O. Ojo, a painting specialist; Mr. Roland Abiodun, an art historian/lecturer; Mr. Babatunde Lawal, Art historian/lecturer; Mr. Agbo Folarin, a London-based Central School-trained specialist in sculptor; Pa Akinola Lasekan, an elder statesman of the arts and renowned portrait artist and teacher. There was also Mr. Akin Euba musicologist/composer who studied in the UK and USA; Mr. Sam Akpabot an American-trained musicologist; Mr. Frank Speed, a cinematographer; Ms. Peggy Harper, a movement/dance researcher in Ethnography and Choreography. Then, there was Ola Rotimi, a Rockefeller Foundation Scholar who studied dramatic literature and playwriting in the USA. These and other experts were absorbed into the African Studies research team. Researchers were charged with leading their respective areas of expertise and encouraging the development of their works with respect to their relevance to the development of Nigerian tradition and culture. These pioneers at University of Ife helped to set the stage for its reputation and accomplishments as a home of tradition and culture – Ife for Culture!

## The Birth of Ori Olokun

As Abiodun Banjo has stated in his article, 'Ori Olokun Art Experimental Workshop: An Epitome of Modernity in Nigerian Visual Art (1968 – 2009)',

> Forty years ago, in 1960, various art workshops were established in Nigeria purposely to develop individual talents and hope that it would set them free from the boredom of formalism. Ideologically, art workshops could be viewed as a veritable tool for liberating captive creativity of Nigerian artists. (Banjo 2013, 130)

Formal Art workshops have been a phenomenal source of liberation for talented artists to work and create freely without being gagged by formalized way of creative expression. They were introduced in Nigeria by organizations such as the missionaries, for example, the 1947 experimental missionary workshop organized by Father Kelly P.M of the African Missionary Society in Oye-Ekiti. Central to the aim of these workshops is indoctrination and conversion by the missionaries. Later educationist got involved in organizing art workshops to develop art forms, one of such is the Mbari, an Artists' movement established in Ibadan in 1961 by Nigerian writers, such as Christopher Okigbo, Demas Nwoko, D.O Fagunwa, J.P Clark, Wole Soyinka as well as South African Ezekiel Mphalele and Austrian anthropologist Ulli Beier, who met occasionally for development and debates. On one of such meetings, Duro Ladipo, the renowned Yoruba travelling theatre writer/director was invited. Ladipo was so impressed by the Ibadan Workshop that he decided to start something similar in Osogbo where he was based. With the help and advice from Beier, Ladipo returned to Osogbo and collaborated with Susan Wenger a visual artist (partner to Ulli Beier), to establish and run the Osogbo Arts Workshop, named Mbari-Mbayo after the Ibadan workshop (1962). The Osogbo Mbari-Mbayo helped explore the inter-relationship in the training of the visual and performing arts.

It was the success of the Osogbo experiment in the development of the art and artists that would later influence the establishment of Ori-Olokun experimental art setup at the University of Ife in 1968. Ori-Olokun Experimental Workshop under the auspices of the African Studies started with a difference, in that it began the formalization of the training process merging the visual and performance arts.

The various art workshops earlier mentioned were established with intentions of benefiting the organizers. Such intentions, for the early missionary workshops, for example, included gaining the trust of the people, getting accepted, influencing the peoples' culture, artistic and creative processes, as well to convert the indigenes. In the workshops, resources were freely given to the participants, but as the saying goes, there is 'no free lunch' anywhere. These workshop organizers had intentions and goals they aim to achieve in the end as Banjo has observed:

> Tracing the origin of art experimental workshops in Nigeria may be difficult without considering the days of the early missionaries and some prominent educational practitioners. It should be noted that some Christian missionaries like Roman Catholics have organized similar workshops as a tool of conversion. (Banjo 2013, 131)

So, the generosity of supplying free materials and other resources to workshop participants came with subtle influences on the artists. This can be observed in the outcome of the products of the Oye Ekiti experimental workshop, where artists were taught and encouraged to use their various African images but their interpretations were influenced by the church. The result can be noticed in some sculptural images that came out of this workshop. The influences deriving from such schools of thought subtly transform the creative processes of the artists as seen in syncretic works such as the popular 'Mother and Child' image in the Yoruba culture translated into Mary and the Child Jesus in some carvings from these workshops. These carvings, with very obvious Yoruba traditional motif, are interpreted into Euro-Christian connotations, such as the Crucifixion, the Last Supper, and other Biblical Saints.

The Ori-Olokun Experimental Workshop differed in that it came at a period when Nigeria was still basking in the euphoria of the 1960 Independence with its high cultural awareness. At that moment, Nigerians were also interested in creating a national identity and dignity. National policies were being formulated, which included arts and cultural policy. The Ori Olokun Workshop was thus established with the intention of developing the arts and culture for Nigerians, who intended to promote freedom of expression through the arts. The idea of the experimental workshop was to create environments that nurtured and developed artists in visual and performance arts under the direction of Nigerian researchers and instructors. However, most writings and publications on the activities resulting from the Ori-Olokun workshop did not reflect the multiple contributions of the different artistic mediums developed during the workshop. Moreover, the influence of the various arts in the workshop on the development of the art in University of Ife is not properly documented. Several writings emphasize Ori-Olokun workshops as visual arts experiments, giving an erroneous impression that it contributed solely to the establishment of the Department of Fine Arts of the University of Ife. However, the reality, on the basis of this author's personal experience, is that Ori-Olokun experimental workshop was an all-encompassing arts experience that contributed to the totality of the development of arts at the University of Ife and to the nation.

## The Workings and Development of Ori Olokun Centre

Michael Crowder, second Director of the Institute of African Studies, co-founded Ori-Olokun as a town-arm of the Research Centre of the Institute to enable the expatriates and Nigerian researchers to get closer to the cultural activities of the Ife people and to the Yoruba tradition at large. The experimental workshop was to encourage, train and develop talented artists nationally who would then participate in the Institute's 'Town & Gown' policy. Crowder also intended the outreach to benefit the university and the community at large in the on-going development of various research projects. In the true spirit of the town and gown policy, researchers of the Institute of African Studies converged at a rented building at Arubidi, Ile-Ife in 1968 to launch what became the Ori-Olokun workshop. Among the researchers was Mr. Ola Rotimi, a playwright/director.

This first meeting brought together invited participants and researchers where the Arts Workshop Project was introduced by members of the Institute of African Studies. Researchers also introduced their various fields of art and research to the artists. At the meeting, the creative talents and interests of participants were explored. As such, this first meeting was a partial audition for acceptance to places in the emerging workshop. The one-week trial that followed started with about 30 participants that included some invited artists from the Mbari-Mbayo workshop who came to participate and to expand their knowledge and experiences. At the end of the trial week, six participants were chosen from the workshop and given positions as Artists-in-Residence to continue with the development of Ori Olokun experimental workshop. These chosen Artists-in-Residence for the training included Ademola Williams (who later became a lecturer in textile, Department of Fine Arts at University of Benin); Rufus

Orisayomi (who became a tutor, film-maker at the University of Benin); Gbade Akintunde (tutor/independent artist, sculptor at Ahmadu Bello University); this author (who became a Senior Arts-Fellow, also at Ahmadu Bello University and later Founder/Artistic Director/Choreographer of London- based Badejo Arts); Rufus Ogundele, and Yinka Adeyemi from the Osogbo Artists (who both became renowned independent artists).

Of all the training sessions, during the workshops, the theatre sessions stood out as all-encompassing. The training in theatre productions led by Ola Rotimi (Himself) were intensive, involving script reading, improvisation exercises, acting techniques and rudiments in technical theatre. There were also voice exercises and training to help individuals. Rotimi paid attention to individuals and encouraged them to develop their different abilities.

## Ola Rotimi (Himself)

Rotimi grew up as a child in a multicultural background born into two distinct traditions: a Yoruba father and an Ijaw Mother. His father, Pa Samuel Gladstone Enitan Rotimi was a man interested in theatre and even directed amateur plays. His mother, Madam Dorcas, also appreciated and loved play productions. So, Ola Rotimi's childhood was not devoid of performances. From an early age, he was cast and acted in amateur plays under his father's direction. He had his early education in schools in the bustling cities of Nigeria, (Lagos and Port Harcourt) where he got good city life experiences. He then departed for the USA where he studied and got his first degree, BA in Fine Arts at Boston University and later obtained an MA from Yale School of Drama. A Rockefeller Foundation Scholar in playwriting and dramatic literature, Rotimi was well prepared and qualified to join the group of enthusiastic scholars. Rotimi came back to an independent Nigeria as a Research Fellow and member of the Institute of African Studies.

At Ori-Olokun, Rotimi and other researchers worked with an array of young talents; amateurs and semi-professionals with raw energy, he had many challenges on his hands. However, he plodded on with determination and focus, and he achieved some measure of success. These groups of artists, some of whom Rotimi scouted for and brought to join the Centre for his production, all went through the training willingly and were shaped, body and mind, to suit his production dreams. Rotimi (Himself) used these training sessions as an opportunity to study and acquire more knowledge of the traditional theatre techniques. By exploring with these artists and local talents, he was able to absorb local ingredients needed for his writings and directing. As time went by, he was able to formulate his directorial philosophy, style and personal technique through these works.

In writing and directing his early plays, such as *The Gods Are Not to Blame* (1968), *Kurunmi* (1969), and *Ovonramwen Nogbaisi* (1971), Rotimi was sharpening his directing and stage-crowd management skills, which he then successfully used in directing his subsequent and other writers' plays. Because of the potency and success of his directorial style, the works of other playwrights that he directed had on them a 'Rotimian signature'. Plays like *Gbekude* by Adegoke Durojaye (1971), *Rererun* by Dejo Okedeji (1973), *The Curse* by Kole Omotoso (1975), *Behold My Redeemer* by Rasheed Gbadamosi (1978), among others, all bear Rotimi's insignia. Rotimi's stage craftsmanship and influence on theatrical productions became so strong that even audiences recognize them in productions other than his own. In the magazine, *KAYODE*, Kola Oyewo's article titled 'Ola Rotimi's Directorial and Managerial Philosophy: An Actor's Experience,' notes that, "whenever he directs another man's play, such play becomes more Rotimi(ian) than the original author(s)" (2000: 47).

As a play director, Ola Rotimi had visual acuity and understanding of the use of crowd on stage. In his plays, crowd scenes are successfully utilized for cultural identity, aesthetics, meaningful understanding, and communication of messages to audiences. He plays with crowd size in his scripting and staging to mirror the typical African natural scenes. The saying 'two is a crowd', a European expression, is un-African, as Rotimi demonstrates. His theatre philosophy influenced his students and other practitioners who had diverse opportunities to work with him on productions. His influences are exhibited in their teaching methods at different institutions in theatre arts programs and in various productions at venues nationally and internationally. Rotimi acquired a systematic style and philosophy in his work that is advanced and recognizable. Yet when one reads the critical writings about playwrights and directors whose works are performed and used in teaching stagecraft in our schools, Rotimi is usually not given his rightful place as an ingenious theatre visionary and authority of note, for his philosophy and style of work. Instead, foreign theatre practitioners and experts with European theatre philosophy are at the top of the lists for teaching materials on script-writing and stage craftsmanship in the country's institutions. This needs to change. It will begin, hopefully, with publications such as this.

## Conclusion

Rotimi created his own identity as a playwright and director with a unique philosophical and practical niche. His works deserve to be studied and taught in our schools in relationship to playwriting and stage craftsmanship relevant to our theatre expressivity. Prior to the rise of Ori-Olokun theatre, English language plays were distant to some audiences in Nigerian communities. With Ola Rotimi's welcomed input into development of the Nigerian theatre, the ordinary person who watched any of his productions was able to enjoy and learn from theatre productions in English. Through Rotimi's production skills, which stem from his research and interactions with tradition and cultural norms of the people, drama productions in English language were brought closer to and understood by average people in the community. Simply put, a Rotimi play can be watched, understood and enjoyed by a cross section of class and cultures of people in our communities.

Additionally, Rotimi also developed practitioners and academics in African theatre expressions across the country. It is about time we decolonize our learning and its processes to free the mind of our young ones, so they too can embrace the creative flow in them. When shall we value our own and recognize self? It is over two decades since Ola Rotimi passed on to the land of our ancestors, and what have we done to further his deep knowledge of theatre-making? I stand for the universality of knowledge, but definitely not to the detriment and debasement of our own contributions to knowledge. We must question the relevance of foreign philosophy in the shaping of our cultural policies and how it affects the development of our theatre practices. As the guided freedom of thought is relevant to the development of minds in the experimental workshops, and have successfully influenced art development today, the same must be done with the learning processes, so that they can creatively shape our tomorrows.

## References

Banjo, Abiodun. 2013. 'Ori Olokun Art Experimental Workshop: An Epitome of Modernity in Nigerian Visual Art (1968 – 2009)'. *International Journal of Humanities and Social Sciences*. Vol. 3 No. 1; January 2013. 130 -138

Oyewo, Kola. 2000. 'Ola Rotimi's Directorial and Managerial Philosophy: An Actor's Experience.' *KAYODE* Magazine. 47.

# CHAPTER SIX

## Ola Rotimi the Playwright, Theatre Director and Lecturer: An Experiential Report

Emmanuel Nwachuku

### Introduction

The legendary Professor Ola Rotimi, also popularly referred to as "Himself", due to his commanding presence, was known to me from 1978 till his departure from this physical world in the year 2000. I was very close not only to him, but also to his wife Hazel and their children; Enitan, Oruene, Abiodun and Kole, with whom I grew up as staff children at the University of Port Harcourt. From November 1984 to October 1985, I became a student in the pioneer set of Ola Rotimi's then Certificate in Theatre Arts at the University of Port Harcourt, and was retained upon graduation from the program as one of the two top products, as an artist-in-residence alongside Oruene Abusi Green for another year.

I was again privileged to become one of the first two products of the eleven months professional certificate programme in Theatre Arts to be admitted to the degree programme from that arrangement in 1986 (the other being Ngozi Maduforo (now Mrs. Orji). Ola Rotimi was thus my mentor and I have greatly admired his creative prowess, the strength of his character, the precision in his utterances and actions as embodied in his commitment to perfection of the performing arts, in both theory and practice.

### Biography of Ola Rotimi

Ola Rotimi is a Nigerian playwright and director of the performing arts with a vision. He was a later arrival on the Nigerian creative scene, the early birds being Hubert Ogunde, J.P. Clark, Wole Soyinka, Duro Ladipo, et al. Ola Rotimi was born on 13th April 1938 in Sapele, by a couple with artistic inclinations. His father, Samuel Gladstone Enitan Rotimi, whose education was up to secondary school, was a Yoruba man and a native of Modakeke in Ile Ife, western Nigeria. His father produced concerts in their neighbourhood as a hobby, and that offered Ola Rotimi his early exposure to the arts of the Theatre. He was cast in a play at the age of four. His mother, Dorcas Adolae Oruene Addo, whose name Oruene he proudly mentioned often, was from southern Nigeria, of the Ijaw speaking Island of Nembe. She also was a leader of a women dance troupe. His father spoke English and Yoruba, while his mother who did not go to school, spoke only Ijaw and pidgin English.

Ola Rotimi spoke English, Yoruba and Ijaw languages and pidgin English which was the favoured language in Rotimi's home. Because his parents migrated a lot, Ola Rotimi attended St. Cyprian's School in Port Harcourt from 1945 to 1949, St Jude's School, Lagos, from 1951 to 1952 and the Methodist Boys High School in Lagos, before travelling to the United States in 1959 to study at Boston University, As a primary and secondary school boy, Ola Rotimi wrote short stories, poems and plays that were sometimes broadcast by Nigerian Broadcasting Corporation (NBC). Though I had seen some of these documents during my interactions with Ola Rotimi, I was unable to access these short stories and poems for the purpose of further details on them in this article, despite all my efforts .

On a scholarship from the federal government of Nigeria. Ola Rotimi graduated in Creative Arts from Boston University, United States of America in 1959, with a major in Directing. Then again with Rockefeller foundation scholarship, Ola Rotimi went on to obtain a master's degree (MA), with major in playwriting at the prestigious Yale University, also in the United States of America. He was, therefore, well equipped for his career as a playwright and director.

Rotimi's contact with Tina Landau (a renowned director) at Yale University greatly influenced his approach to play production. The skills put on display, the style and result realised by Landau at the instance of directing Ola Rotimi's maiden play, *Our Husband Has Gone Mad Again* (1977), made a great impression on Ola Rotimi and was reflective in his works. Ola Rotimi, in his many interviews, comments that other playwrights like William Shakespeare, Eugene O'Neill and Arthur Miller also made an impression on him, particularly Shakespeare's characterization through dialogue techniques.

## Ola Rotimi as a Playwright

Rotimi wrote two kinds of plays, historical plays and satires, writing in both tragic and comic genres. A majority of Rotimi's plays are written, using realism as artistic style. He weaves most of his plays around historical events as seen in

*Kurumi (1971), Ovonramwen Nogbaisi* (1974), and *Hopes of The Living Dead (1986).* The language of most of his plays are lucid English with Nigerian indigenous exclamations and expressions successfully. He successfully captures characters through language, because he makes different characters in his plays speak according to the extent of their education or exposure. This is also applied even in plays like *Ovonramwen Nogbaisi* and *Kurunmi* (both historical homonymous tragedies), where the real characters were known to have spoken only in Yoruba language that is translated to English language in the play text, but retaining the essential Yoruba proverbs with translations for the benefit of the audience - the reason why he forbids his actors from using a tribal accent in delivering their lines.

Rotimi posits (during my private lines rehearsal with him for the role of King Odewale in his *The Gods Are Not To Blame* in 1985) that a person cannot have an accent in his native language. He structures his dialogues with a heavy overtone of proverbial speech structure, as common in most Nigerian languages of the many ethnic nationalities in the country for the purpose of capturing the texture and real meanings of African speech patterns.

Despite what appears to be complexity in his use of language, the language in Rotimi's plays are easy to assimilate and designed to suit the dichotomy of the Nigerian audience, which is invariably of mixed ethnic nationalities, and an international audience at large. He also had a technique of building Nigerian languages into his contemporary dialogue as is the practice of Nigerians in real life and this is traceable to his father's production style. Turner is of the view in his discourse on the role of language narratives that,

> Narrative can be described as a means of making sense of our social world, and sharing that 'sense' with others ... Its universality underlies its intrinsic place in human communication of which every society has developed its own style over the years that are meaningful in their performance culture. (1993, 68)

Rotimi's family language during his childhood was a mix of English, pidgin English, Yoruba and Ijaw and it came naturally to him that if this arrangement worked in his smaller family, why not in the larger family of his dramatic creations.

Ola Rotimi in his scripted and practical creation of scenes made deliberate efforts to break away from the popular European proscenium stage approach to presentations. He showed a preference for thrust and arena theatre settings. He believed and demonstrated that the traditional African communal theatre audience participation in the performance was more communicative and experiential to the audience. He, therefore, rejected the fourth wall convention in totality and beyond sitting his audience close to his actors, he wrote for his actors to make their entries with lines from the aisles in the auditorium or from among the audience, and in a play like his *Voices and Sacrifice*, staged at the Crab Theatre in 1985, all his actors emerge from among the seated audience. When the auditorium is unable to accommodate the audience, Ola Rotimi will seat excess audience on parts of the performance space/stage, as is applicable in traditional African theatre.

As a regular lead actor on several of his casts from 1984 to 1989 this was a constant repeated experience at the University of Port Harcourt theatre known as the Crab, and many other theatres performed on tours all over Nigeria during my years of training under Ola Rotimi, within which period I obtained a professional certificate in theatre Arts (Acting track), worked as an artiste in residence and advance to do my first three years on the BA Theatre Arts programme (Directing track). His standards then distinguish his product from later products of same university, some years after his departure and that of his direct products. A similar experience was expressed by Barclays Ayakoroma in his keynote lecture, 'Theatre Practice in Nigeria: To be or not to be', which he delivered at the 2012 celebrations of the International Theatre Day, which was organised by National Association of Nigerian Theatre Arts Practitioners (NANTAP), at the Cyprian Ekwensi Cultural Centre Port Harcourt, Nigeria, on Tuesday, March 27, 2012. The "Certificate in Theatre Arts (CTA) programme of the University of Port Harcourt", according to Ayakoroma,

> was conceptualized by Rotimi as a professional programme, where graduands were expected to go for a one-year industrial attachment before proceeding to the degree programme. The auditions for admission into the programme was very painstaking, and created quite an entertainment for the university community. Somehow, the process has since been jettisoned and admission to the programme is now being handled just like other Basic Studies programmes… (Ayakorama 2012)

In my final year of study in 1989/1990 academic year, Rotimi transferred his services to the Obafemi Awolowo University Ile-Ife, but left us in the care of Dr. Carroll Dawes, an expatriate of Jamaican origin, who on her part had retired from the Edna Manley College of the Performing and Visual Arts, Kingston,

Jamaica. Dawes had served a contract at the University of Ibadan, another at the Amadu Bello University in Zaria, Nigeria, and finally arriving at the age of 74 years in 1988 to the University of Port Harcourt, where she headed and groomed the students and staff till her departure to England in 1992.

## Experiencing Ola Rotimi as a Director

Some schools of thought have popularized the perception of Ola Rotimi as an avowed Marxist. Rotimi's directorial style and the image which he carved out for himself in the theatre is in fact postulated by many dramatists to allude to the tradition of the singular "great writer" and "great director". He is often presented as an individualist, not democratic nor a team worker, a trend said to be found propagated in his directed plays by his critics. This assumption is easy for many to posit as a summation of Rotimi's personality particularly because it has been propagated as a truism by many scholars. On a closer scrutiny, however, the assumption may prove to be totally unfounded, especially to anyone who was close to him and could see the motivations and team work approach of the perfectionist that Ola Rotimi was all through his life.

"Himself", Rotimi's given nickname, arose due to the fact that despite his deficiency in physical height (being a little above 4ft in height), Rotimi had such a robust and intimidating personality that he appeared to turn anyone around him into a dwarf by his superior intellect and quickness of mind. He was strong-willed and almost impossible to derail once he sets himself a target. He was largely perceived to be a dictator, and had the ability to withhold his smile or laughter even in the event of something that makes people around roll on the floor with laughter, this is despite being amused and having a good laugh later in private or company of his family or disciples, both instances of which I was a daily participant.

Rotimi was not seen as a dictator to many who worked closely with him. He simply resented people with no initiative and will readily think for them and direct them on what to do to expedite the job at hand. He was always pleased with those who were able to discern the purpose of what he commanded them to do and he actually welcomed polite and constructive objection to his instructions and was known to accept and apply better ideas from even the most junior of his students and openly acknowledge that contribution and the contributor. He thrived in team work and was quick to identify people with leadership qualities and put them in charge of the many small teams he creates in a work group, cast, crew or class. He then moved the slower minded around, using his chosen team leaders. He is followed by his loyalists like a religious leader even after his death.

**Directing Techniques of Ola Rotimi:** The first thing that comes to mind when thinking of Rotimi's directing techniques is his use of crowd without masking anyone on stage. Ola Rotimi paints pictures with the crowd, creating and collapsing tabloids in very rapid succession and with a constant change in rhythms and tempo even in his absurdist play, *Holding Talks* (1979). He manipulates crowd to give derived emphases to specific characters or actions in every movement, creating fluid pictures with depth in the process. His crowd placements also communicate key moods of the moment, like solidarity, polarity, conflict, etc. Crowd placement and movement in an Ola Rotimi's production can communicate the massage of the play to a deaf audience. Ola Rotimi used levels, he varied the speed of dramatic actions, he applied triangles and semi-circle formations, he used multiple actions on stage and it was impossible for masking to occur on his set, or for a pivot stage to flaw his stage balance, as we experienced at the University of Lagos main bowl 1986 performance of *Hopes of the Living Dead* on a national tour, as he tested his work with the pivot mechanism available at that two thousand and two hundred capacity proscenium theatre with a predominant apron.

As a master director that he proved to be, Rotimi successfully manipulates large crowd on the small stage of the Crab theatre at University of Port Harcourt, creating realistic and appealing stage pictures even in that tight enclosure. The use of crowd is a signature of most Rotimi plays, such as *Kurumi, If… A Tragedy of the Ruled*, *The Gods Are Not To Blame* and *Ovonranwem Nogbaisi.* He uses crowd to emphasize the strength of the masses. An example of this is the panic situation in the hospital attack scene to eject the wards D and H leprosy patients in *Hopes of the Living Dead*, which was foiled by their organised resistance. He also uses triangles, semi-circles and angle formations, plus multiple levels and speed in collapsing and changing tabloids to create a picturization that does not mask any actor at any moment in the performance nor permit the loss of stage balance even for a moment. This is a most uncommon art, even among famed directors worldwide. The crowd is used as a symbol of unity and strength, hence Ikoli Harcourt Whyte was motivated back into action by the crowd via the songs of the inmates, after his second unsuccessful encounter with the hospital authorities, which left him depressed and defeated.

**Rotimi's Artist Training Techniques**: For 1985 performances of *The Gods Are Not To Blame*, Rotimi took his cast and crew to see where the three footpaths meet near Ede, then to the shrine of Ogun and the shrine of Osun all in Oyo state of Nigeria. In *Hopes of the Living dead*, Ola Rotimi took cast and crew to the now demolished Port Harcourt General Hospital wards D and H, then located at Moscow/Agrey Road and also to the former infectious diseases hospital (IDH), now primary health centre at Aluu in University of Port Harcourt host Community. These guided excursions, he said, were to enable cast and crew have mental pictures of the actual environment and culture when they re-create the events on stage.

This author played the following roles in the listed plays under the directions of Ola Rotimi: Hamidu Gidadu, in *IF… 1987 performance.* The character, Raman Lejoka Brown in *Our Husband Has Gone Mad Again* – 1989 multiple performances, Odewale in *The Gods Are Not To Blame* – 1985 to 1988 repertory performances, Editor in *Hopes of the Living Dead* -1985 and 1986 performances, and Dr Ilori in his touring production of Rasheed Gbadamosi's *Behold my Redeemer* in 1987 touring performances directed by Rotimi.

In *Behold My Redeemer* tour in 1987, principal cast consisted of Dike Nwachuku and Bob-Manuel Udokwu doubled for the character Dr Ilori. Mildred Iweka and Esther Roberts doubled for the character Shijuwomi, while Columbus Irisoanga and Ejike Asiegbu doubled for the character Doctor. Rotimi took the principal cast to spend a month attending ward rounds with medical students, nurses, and doctors at the Rumuigbo psychiatric hospital in Port Harcourt, Nigeria. He also took the cast to the Harbour Road prisons lunatics section and then assigned the two lead characters (Dike Nwachuku and Mildred Iweka) and their doubles to follow and study specific mad people on the streets. This author was assigned to a lunatic nicknamed, "Prof" at the Choba market, in Obio Akpo LGA of Rivers state, and followed him around daily from 9am to 6pm for two weeks, which gave him the experience for memory recall in portraying the character on stage. This was a Jerzy Growtosky's technique of developing a character adopted by Ola Rotimi.

For academic clarity on a common misconception, it is necessary to posit here that Grotowsky is the exponent of observation theory in acting, while Constantine Stanislavsky on another hand advocated living the part as a technique for his experience and memory recall theory, the two theories and their implication dwell on memory recall, but are very different in context. Rotimi did not require his cast to live the life of lunatics, they only observed without contact as in Grotowski's technique, but in Stanislavsky's technique, the theorist is recorded to have made his wife live amongst prostitutes, dress, eat and act like them for six months in other to play the character on stage. What is however not stated is if his wife also had to practice the act of prostitution.

## Ola Rotimi's Dramaturgy: Two Case Studies as Interpreted on Stage by Rotimi

***Hopes of the Living Dead* (1986 & 1988 performances)**: The play was first titled *When the Dead Awaken* in its 1985 maiden performance at the Crab theatre, University of Port Harcourt and was quickly re-titled within the week of its first staging. As part of the premiere cast, this author was a double cast for the role of Editor, played by Niyi Coker. The production of March 1986 being referred to in this paper, was also staged at the same venue and was an improvement of the former, serving that year as the university's convocation play, which saw Ola Rotimi act on stage as the superintendent of police, because the actor cast to play the role (Victor Eriabe) failed to turn up for performance, due to post convocation celebrations.

Harcourt Whyte the leader of the Lepers (played by Columbus Irisoanga) was an embodiment of purposeful and self-sacrificial leadership desired for the greatness of a nation. His character was, however, not allowed to tower above those he led. He mobilises and co-ordinates other characters, fitting in as a people grown leader, with his popular refrain, "Each one, tell one", towards a common goal and eventual victory over their predicament. He encourages them to stick together with the lines,

> We must stand together, children of our fathers. Not apart. The day the children of the porcupine made bond to drift apart: one, going this way, a mouse; the other going that way, a bush rat, is the day both mouse and bush rat become food for the cats, together then, we move… (Rotimi 1986, 111)

Another significant personality in this play is Hannah, (played by Oruene Abusi Green). The real Hannah in the historical event did not join the Lepers until they located to the Uzuakoli lepers' colony, but Ola Rotimi puts Hannah on stage to achieve gender balance in leadership and show the strength of the female supportive role to a leader. She is resolute, positive, reliable and stubborn, especially when incoherence threatens her group. For the third time, Ola Rotimi creates a female character that is not domesticated as he did in the character of

'Liza' in *Our Husband Has Gone Mad Again* and 'Betty' in *If…A Tragedy of the Ruled.* Hannah is a dominant character, indicative of what stance the playwright wishes future Nigerian women to take in nation-building according to his brief to the cast.

Other notable characters include CC (played by Nathanael Egba), Nweke (played by Jaja Adafe) and Nweke (played by Yei Ruben), who all represented good followership. Matron (played by Lola Oluyode/Stella Osuji), The Senior Medical Officer (played by Peter Feuser) and the Superintendent of Police (played by Ola Rotimi), a representation of uncaring and cruel government official, interested only in their selfish purposes. The Editor, Julius Wadimi Biagbozo (played by this author) reflects some members of society who cannot rise above self in their commitment to a legitimate course. For example, he goes into a drunken stupor and eruptive temper, because a letter drafted by him to the hospital authorities was criticised by a group member.

Catechist (played by Enitan Godfrey) is the critic of the letter drafted by Editor and is a pessimistic, greedy and selfish character. The editor was about the only one in the group, however, who saw sanity in doctor Ferguson's leprosy experiment in a regular hospital, which earned him the title of "mad Scots man". The Catechist and Editor are later brought to a physical confrontation which purged them of their vices as the people were made to be their judges and hand them strict penalties that were forgiven when they begged for forgiveness. This made them rededicate themselves to the course of the group. The message put to the audience by the playwright is that the people can prevail on their rulers through solidarity of purpose and this is the elixir for a society to make progress.

The play made use of upwards of fifteen Nigerian ethnic languages applied in the crowd of over fifty inmates, particularly, Hausa, Igbo, Yoruba, Fulani, Tiv, Uhrobo, Ikwerre, Efik and Ibibio, etc. So language in the play serves as both a vehicle for carrying the theme of ethnic unity across to the audience and also serves as tool for the realization of personalities and emotions of the characters, which elucidates empathy in the audience. The dialogue in the play breaks into a confused atmosphere regularly, this is purely a design by the writer to tell the Nigerian populace that ethnicity and tribalism are the major threats to unity in the country. Repeatedly in the play, the characters break into speaking their individual native vernacular when faced with a challenge. It is fascinating, however, to see how the playwright uses the actors as interpreters to one another to solve the communication problems created, hence the refrain of the line, "each one, tell one" (forewarning that something important is about to be said and should be communicated to all). This occurs right throughout the play.

Use of songs is another regular technique of communication applied by Rotimi in his plays. The Christian religious songs of hope composed by Ikoli Harcourt Whyte (who was a music composer and choirmaster) is used through the play to communicate developing events and create the relevant moods. The songs are used to heighten the aesthetic value of the production. Rendered in all four voice parts of soprano, alto, tenor and bass and in a good tempo, the songs are intended to have an overwhelming vocal impact on the audience and emphasize the message of solidarity and is also used to explain the actions of the moment when they are rendered, as experience in his staged interpretations of his plays, especially as directed by him.

***If... A tragedy of the Ruled* (1979 performance)**: The play, a political satire that emerged on the eve of Nigeria's return to civil rule in 1979, is a tragic depiction of the dilemma of a people in search of purposeful leadership. With a setting in the low-income residential area of Diobu in Port Harcourt, Rivers state Nigeria, the play depicts the realities of the existence in Nigeria of the common man, with a warning to Nigerians and politicians, in particular, to place their priorities right if the nation is to positively develop. While *Hopes of the Living Dead* preaches the abandonment of ethnicity, for national unity, *If...* is preoccupied with persons and human problems that inhibit democracy. Rotimi was cited to have said, "The substance of *If...* is ostensibly political, but not partisan" (*Sunday Tide*: 3rd June 1979, 11).

The characters in *If... A Tragedy of the Ruled,* fall within the dramatic style of realism, as is usual with most Rotimi plays. The characters are real and well-developed representations of regular people the audience can easily identify with and a true reflection of the Nigerian society. Ola Rotimi states to his 1986 directing class, that he spends months to study real people of choice for the purpose of recreating them in his dramatic creations and this helps to make his characters real and believable. Actions in the play *If... A Tragedy of the Ruled* as directed and staged at the University of Port Harcourt in 1987, flow into each other in progression and are simultaneous, without demarcation between time, space and action. This invokes an atmosphere of typical urban life in a low-income locale. This is what Rotimi describes as "...convoluting concusses of juxtaposed variegated happenings..." (*Hopes of the Living Dead* Production programme, February 8, 1985, 3).

The most prominent of the languages used in *If...* is the Port Harcourt variety of the Pidgin English, amidst other ethnic languages and English language. The target audience is, therefore, the common man in whose hands the power to elect leaders at the polling centres should rest. Music is also used in the usual Rotimi style to emphasize religious overtone and spiritual intervention expectations of the Nigerian public. The songs range from popular highlife tunes to religious songs, rendered primarily in the dominant ethnic languages of Ogoni, Ijaw, Kalabari and Ikwerre, found in the Rivers state of Nigeria.

In this 1987 performance of *If... A tragedy of the Ruled,* Papa (played by Nwonosike Okocha) is the monumental figure around whom other characters revolve. He is a retired teacher who commands great respect in the neighbourhood and beyond, as a living image of the dying values of the Nigerian public. Onyema Ejindu (played by Edem Nutsukpo/Clever MacAmingo) is the tragic victim of society's decadence and neglect. He is a little boy of about eleven years old, son of a single mother, Sister Chinwe (played by Ngozi Iwuanyanwu/ Timi Zuofa), who buries her sorrows in Christian religious extremes. Onyema who has just passed the federal common entrance represents the promise of the future. His name in the Igbo language is an abbreviation of "Onyemaechi" meaning; who knows tomorrow? and "Ejindu" do we hold life? He is, therefore, a living question on the hope of future generation of Nigerians and posterity. And on another hand, we have the Landlord (played by Ejike Asiegbu) as a representation of the property class, that is greedy for money and political power.

There are representations of different ethnic groups and strata, typical of an average Nigerian urban area, and identifiable by their actions and reactions to events. Some notable characters include Banji Falegan (played by Igbanibo Saki/Michael Ogbolosingha), a lawyer, who is representative of the liberals in society. Hamidu Gidadu (played by this author/Jaja Adafe). He is a youth corp doctor, that is a representation of a left-wing shade of opinion in the country. He is talkative and grumbles about what government (others) have not done, without necessarily doing anything himself, other than enjoy the rhetorics of his own grumbling. When confronted with the death of Onyema, he shifts all blame to the government and takes no blame for not having any personal first aid materials in his medical kit. He says, "Allah, as a trained doctor, I am useless here. I will never forgive this country for that... (1983, 79).

Betty Oviamwen (Catherine Campbell/Immaculata Chikeka) is a societal victim who is portrayed as so downtrodden that she would survive by any means, including selling her body to the Landlord for rent relief, turns out to be the most realistic and rational citizen in the play, with the right action for the right situation. Betty who is an illiterate and communicates only in pidgin English is pragmatic. Despite her sexual affair with the Landlord, she alone finds the courage to confront the Landlord on principles of the dehumanizing treatment meted out to Garuba Kazuare (played by Maxwell Esono). Even when Onyema was found at the point of death, it was she who brushed aside the grumblings of Hamidu and did a practical thing of putting Onyema on her back to carry him to the distant hospital. She demonstrates to Hamidu and to the audience that the right action and not words are what is needed at the right time to deal with emergencies.

The lowest group in the play are represented by Garuba, Mama Ukot (played by Marbel Nlumanze/Christiana Okon), Fisherman (played by Dagogo Diminas-Jack/ Michael Ogbolosingha) and Mama Rosa (Catherine Campbell/ Rhoda Boro). Their characters are all a reflection of the dehumanizing effect of capitalist governance on society. These "wretched of the earth" as Frantz Fanon calls them, are found at the bottom of the social ladder. The pluralistic characterization in *If...* therefore, provides ample room for all strata of society to have their views expressed in accordance with the myth of open government or democracy.

In an interview with *Sunday Tide*, Ola Rotimi, speaking on the death of Onyema and the consequent mental collapse of Papa postulates that,

> With yesterday blanked out (Papa), tomorrow blanked out (Onyema), today becomes a ghoulish nightmare of uncertainties and meaning-lessness, engulfing the youth as its worst victims. Here-in lies my apprehension. I wouldn't say the message. Apprehension is a more appropriate word for in this face may be the irrevocable curse of Nigeria from 1979 onward- If... (*Sunday Tide* 3 June, 1979,11).

This summation by Rotimi is so apt and real even today bin Nigerian politics when we reflect upon the resent End SARS riots of 2020 in Nigeria, Indeed an "...irrevocable curse of Nigeria from 1979 onward..." (ibid).

Onyema died in protest against the societal ills. First, he sees the arrogance politicians personified in the character Landlord, who is consequently disgraced by deaf and dumb Garuba, who threw away Landlord's birthday gift for Mama, because of his callous manner of presentation. The consequent return with political thugs to dehumanize Garuba, broke Onyema and he withdrew to himself and forgot to put on his shirt or keep warm as an asthma patient and the crises he suffers after several hours of such exposure and shock suffocates him to death. Papa on the other hand had put so much hope in Onyema as his future, so that his death causes his insanity. Rotimi's dramaturgy gives a clear view of his thinking and values for humanity.

## Author's Experience of Ola Rotimi as a Lecturer/Teacher

After a lecture in my second-year degree programme, in the then uncompleted building of Ofrima hall at the University of Port Harcourt, Prof Rotimi in his usual style asked several students to wait and took his time to talk to each privately. When it was the turn of this author, he advised him to stop holding on rigidly to the writing of Oscar Brockett and start forming his own opinion of the arts. He opined that the author's generation should tell the truth of the African origins of theatre and expose the fact that a well-developed theatre existed in Egypt in the Abydos passion plays 2000 years before the European lie of world theatre origins being synonymous with the origin of theatre in Greece, through the worship of the Greek god of wine and fertility, Dionysus in 6th century BC.

When this author asked why he always found time to talk to each student after class, unlike other lecturers, his response was, "I am a teacher and not a lecturer", and when asked the difference, he further opined that, "a lecturer lectures and gives reference then departs; a teacher goes further to study each student and finds time to pull up the slow and encourage the fast learners as the teacher considers everywhere a classroom and tries to know every student as a person. But to a lecturer, a student is just a matriculation number". Rotimi was so intimate, he usually called every one of his students by first, middle and last names and had a pet name for most, hence this author was nicknamed "Ebube Dike, Son of Oscar Brockett " (for excessively quoting Oscar Brockett).

Another example of technique used by Ola Rotimi to engage students' attention and impact them is captured in an incident in the same classroom during this author's third year of the B.A. programme. He came to class that morning and as was his tradition, he chanted, "Pedidentum ad hominin-tudinem..." and the class responded, "Querentum". Meaning, "Approach as if in search of...?" and response, "knowledge". He then called for dictionaries and students all held up their Dictionaries. Next, he called for Bibles or Quran. If you have none of these or you are more than five minutes late, you cannot enter his class as a student. Having confirmed each student had at least one of these holy books and dictionary that he often quoted during lectures, Rotimi then wrote on the board, "Drama and Dramatic". Turning around, he saw an imaginary snake and shouted snake with fear on his face, and in a second the cowards fled from the class through the windows, while the brave grabbed objects to kill the snake. He then told the class to sit down as there was no snake. Sequel to this, he educated the class, that dramatic refers to an action that has dramatic elements but is neither planned nor rehearsed, while drama, scripted or improvised, is a rehearsed enactment of a dramatic event that communicated a message. This differentiation between drama and dramatic that other lecturers have explained elaborately without making clear sense was clearly understood by every member of the class present that day. Such practical methods of teaching were utilized by Rotimi on a regular basis.

## Conclusions

This paper is an encyclopaedic or almanac entry for someone who is interested to access general knowledge on Ola Rotimi, first as a person, then a lecturer and also as a dramatist. It has, therefore, been an attempt to give a reportage and an insight to the person of Ola Rotimi through personal experiences of this author. His relevance to the academia, and the techniques by which he distinguished himself as a playwright, director, teacher and mentor. This is in the hope that some of his fewer known methods may be revealed to academic and commercial practitioners of the performing arts. Comparative literature reviews with other contemporaries have not been in view for this study, because the objective is not to make a thesis submission laden with theorising and problematising the work of this great writer and theatre practitioner with an in-depth academic analysis. This article stops at how Ola Rotimi is perceived as a mentor, through the views of this author, and provides a stepping stone for further studies towards positioning his works in literary perspectives and world view.

Ola Rotimi brings out students' capabilities and sometimes predicts what they are supposed to become in life. He told this author that he must end up becoming a lecturer and the response was a loud "God forbid" given how poorly lecturers were paid at the time in Nigeria. Rotimi laughed and further told this author that his multi-talents in the arts point him towards teaching and he will remind him when he becomes a lecturer. As predicted, in 1999, when this author was lecturing at the Lagos State University, Rotimi sent him message to stand-by for a production, and then reminded him that his prediction had come to pass. Unfortunately, that production never held, as 'the man died'. That is the kind of teacher/lecturer Professor Ola Rotimi was. He accurately predicted careers for many of his students as affirmed by several former students.

With regards to his directing techniques, the most extraordinary things about his directing include allocating days of rehearsals to what happens backstage, detailing every movement back stage and costume placements and changing. He further holds vigorous rehearsals of set changing, usually ending with doing it in total darkness or with blindfolds as was experienced in 1986 production of *Hopes of the Living Dead* tour preparations and 1987 performance of If…*A Tragedy of the Ruled,* at the University of Port Harcourt convocation arena.

Rotimi also made all students in the department learn songs from all over the world compulsorily every Wednesday for the purpose of enriching their ability to find relevant songs for all productions that may arise, during or after studentship. He records on tape how he wants all actors with speaking roles to pronounce words, taking time to explain the meaning of each line in the context applied in the scene so the individual actor can work with the tape privately, but with liberty to adapt same to their individual speech pattern provided that the intent of the spoken line is not compromised. Beyond all this, Ola Rotimi, as earlier mentioned in this article, puts the observation and memory recall techniques of Jerzy Grotowski into use most effectively as an actor training technique.

In conclusion, it may be appropriate to consider the implications of one of his most popular statements, as contained in the director's charge to artistes in the production programme/pamphlet for *Hopes of the Living Dead* (1985). Rotimi charged the cast and crew on the first day of cast meeting thus,

> I want this production to achieve a convoluting concuss of juxtaposed variegated happening. My bargain is that of the devil, you offer me your bodies and I insist on your soul. Till the production is over, tell your grandmother not to lose a toenail, there is no room for excuses. Good night. (3)

Indeed, he kept to his word, not only in this particular production, but in all of his endeavours and creative interactions as a playwright, director and lecturer. There was never a room for excuses or compromise. However, there was always plenty of time to encourage the weak and slow or pull the smart to greater speed and intellect.

## References

Ayakoroma, Barclays. 2012. 'Theatre Practice in Nigeria: To be or not to be'. A Keynote Lecture, at Cyprian Ekwensi Cultural Centre Port Harcourt. March 27.

Rotimi, Ola. 1983. *If… A Tragedy of the Ruled.* Ibadan: Heinemann Educational Books.

__________ 1988. *Hopes of the Living Dead.* Ibadan: Spectrum Books Limited.

__________ 1985. *Hopes of the Living Dead*, Production programme, February 8.

__________1986. If… *A Tragedy of the Ruled*, Production Pamphlet, March.

*Sunday Tide*, 3rd June, 1979, 11.

Turner, V. 1986. *The Anthropology of Performance.* New York: PAJ.

# CHAPTER SEVEN

## Looking Back: Ola Gladstone Rotimi (A Tribute)

*Bimbo Manuel*

*...[T]he blind man bearing a lantern;*
*the lamp is not for him to see,*
*it is for you who have eyes...*

His generation of scholars and dramatists, was enigmatic but he defined them all – enigma who defied definition. He was a paradox, at once fatherly yet aloof; incomparable teacher who had little patience for the thick; an eagle who pretended not to see. Ola Rotimi.

My time with Professor Ola Rotimi was very short, compared to the advantage my contemporaries at the University of Port Harcourt had to get inside his very private world. He however affected my life in such ways that few outside of my immediate family have. It was impossible to meet Ola Rotimi and not be influenced.

Writing anything about 'Prof', as we all called him, defies articulation. Such is the greatness of The Man in the eyes of those of us who had constant encounters with him, even if mine was for a brief spell. He shaped me. Because he was, I became an actor, a writer and director. If I have also been a disciplined professional in the estimation of my colleagues in the industry, it is because I met Ola Rotimi. This is therefore not an academic paper. It is my memory of HIM, who lives still. When I think of him these days, two phrases instantly pop to mind – drama, discipline and in my view, these encapsulate what he stood for.

The first time I set eyes on Professor Ola Rotimi was sometime in September, 1985 - I am uncertain about the exact date now. Armed with recommendation letters from people he knew and obviously thought kindly of, Chief Yomi Obileye, of blessed memory, 'Baba Agba' Jimi Solanke and a few others, I arrived at the University of Port Harcourt PS Auditorium for the audition that would decide if I met the cut for entrance into one of his incredible educational creations, the Certificate in Theatre Arts (CTA) Course, a crash program that compressed the department's regular 4-year Creative Arts program of the University into one year of high-press learning.

I had never met him before, I had no idea what he looked like, I had barely ever heard of him, understandably, coming from a background in radio and television. Someone pointed him out to me, seated at the heart of the press of bodies of his assistants and men and women of all ages trying to register for the audition. He sat still, totally unaffected by the mill around him, quiet, yet an aura of authority that demanded respect, surrounded him. 'Good morning, sir…' No reaction, just a cock of his head of thick, full hair. The keen eyes behind the thick lenses of his glasses piercing through me, questioning, almost as if I was interrupting his meditation. I handed him the bunch of enveloped letters and one more look at me after quickly glancing through them, he waved me to join the long queue to write my name. He gave nothing away.

I applied to train as a director and I did not know there were surprises waiting for me. At that point, I had become uncertain that I wanted to continue. He never related with me on any personal level again after that, till the end of my course when he gave me his verdict of me. As an actor, his *The Gods Are Not To Blame* was the very first drama I was exposed to in performance, playing 'Narrator' and doubling as one of the 'Chiefs'. Of course, that got me into instant trouble with him, on many fronts. The most unforgettable was in his office where he had invited us for text and character work. I cannot tire of telling the story and even my family has heard it a few times to a good laugh. It was my first real lesson in theatre process and discipline.

He had given us the text a few weeks before then with clear instructions to make sure we had our lines before rehearsals. Like most of my green horn mates, I had somehow managed to get my lines so when he invited us for text and character work, I did not think it necessary to carry the script. No one should blame me, no one told me I needed to, after all, I was coming from television and chomping at the bit, struggling to understand why no one had started to say anything to us yet about being a director on television. Such was my ignorance of the theatre and how it was different from television.

He had a class that morning and we had to wait for him to finish. His Office Assistant said 'Prof' had asked us to please go to the small cafe in the complex to get something to eat while we waited. My first experience of that side of him as a caring father and a considerate gentleman. It was an act so courteous, so human, I found it confusing because so totally contradictory. You cannot blame me. My view of him up to that day was of an austere man, stingy with everything, especially praise and consideration.

I had started to attend his Directing Major classes and to me at that time, Professor Ola Rotimi was not human; he was extra-terrestrial, removed, so intellectual yet such easy style of passing on what he knew. He was incapable of this sort of gesture. He was godlike. So, we all cautiously ordered simple snacks and a drink each. It didn't come to much and the Office Assistant paid instantly. We had barely finished eating when word came that he was ready and waiting for us in one of the classrooms. We marched in confidently, ready to show him how prepared we were. He had a large tape recorder and the script on the table, he greeted us jovially, even cracked a joke followed by an apology. It was not 'Prof'. This was a kind teacher, a generous mentor, a father. Then he requested for our copies of the text. Only one person brought his, Bob-Manuel Udokwu. For a few seconds, the room was quiet, the air thick with tension while he stared at us with that famous piercing look that told you without him saying a word that you were in big trouble.

Then he gently queried if we understood what our omission meant. He did not need to explain. We knew. Then with a deliberateness that made his dagger words even more piercing, he gave a piece of his mind - I would learn later that it was just a small piece. He dispatched us with such controlled rage that brooked no explanation or apology. He demanded that we should all ensure that we refunded the money he spent on us for the snacks! We barely scraped the refund together, less sixty kobo or something as inconsequential and handed it to the Office Assistant.

It was a bit of a walk from his office in the faculty to the theatre and we set out on the long walk, all of us, apart from Bob, a pitiable lot. We had gone only a short distance when the Office Assistant rode up on his rickety motorcycle to inform us that 'Prof' said we could not leave till we refunded the whole amount! Somehow, we did. It was another side of him, Professor Ola Rotimi. He regarded misdemeanours dimly and would not ever show it leniency in any way.

As I would find later, the demand for excellence, all or nothing, ruled everything he did. He did not spare even himself. He rarely praised anything or anyone except the exceptional. I do not know many who are more measured with commendation but when he did, it was as extravagant as his vitriol. It was only the beginning of my relationship with him. With the benefit of hindsight, I think, the fact that he knew Yomi Obileye, Jimi Solanke and others who recommended me made me of particular interest to him.

We played *The Gods Are Not To Blame* several times and many of my mates commended my performance. However, all I could see was his dark gaze, each time he looked in my direction in spite of his warm words before each show. I could not help thinking that he held a very low view of me and probably regretted admitting me. On one of the return trips from playing in Port Harcourt town, I asked the Stage Manager, a classmate of mine, if I could be allowed to drop off on the way. He refused. I was very angry because I was definitely not looking forward to the long walk back from school to my room in the village. We had a bit of a row in the bus and of course, Prof got to hear.

He explained to me that the Stage Manager was his representative and any and every disobedience to him was a direct challenge to the Director, himself! I was therefore suspended for two whole weeks! I was not allowed in or around the theatre until the end of my suspension. He stopped short of a total school ban! He was livid.

## My second lesson in the theatre

At that time of course, I had given up on having any personal relationship with him. I was sure he did not like me. Then it was time to present his newest play, *Hopes of the Living Dead*. We were only the second set of casts to ever play it. As you would have guessed, of all the roles, I got the one that he himself had played before, the 'Superintendent'. Learning the lines of the 'Narrator' and the few mutterings of the 'Chief' was one thing, mastering the hefty lines of the 'Superintendent' was a task fit only for the tested and I wondered then how he expected anyone, me, least of all, to memorize it all and perform it.

I had never had to do that in my life and all I wanted was television – I was still struggling to come to terms with understanding that I came in for theatre and not television directing as I dreamed. But I must do it. You did not engage Ola Rotimi when he gave you a task. I remember that on the first page of the script, in his charge to the performers, he had written and I paraphrase, '…I drive the Devil's bargain, you offer yourself, I demand your soul…' It made my heart sink.

Like a few others, I did not have my lines on the day rehearsals opened but he permitted us to work with our scripts, especially to enable us take down our blocking. He dropped it lightly a few times that on a given date, he would not permit scripts anymore. Everyone worked feverishly and some managed to finally master their lines. I could not. It felt like I was the only one speaking in the entire production. I was overwhelmed and that made it more difficult for me to memorize the lines.

Day. Yes, I was not ready. Everyone was anxious for me. Prof was perched in his usual seat high up at the back of the auditorium, waiting, watching as I bungled line after line. The auditorium held its breath. Then he rose, slowly and approached the stage. He told the other actors to take their seats. I was the only one standing. I felt lonely, naked, all eyes on me. I knew I had given it my best shot but clearly it was not going to be enough for this man who never seemed to understand how hard we had all tried. Then he plowed into me. People who timed it estimated my crucifixion to have lasted about twenty-five minutes. It felt like twenty-five days. I had never been spoken to in such manner nor ever since. I told myself not to feel the pain but focus on his mastery of the English language instead. I do not think I would have been able to bear it otherwise.

I was given ten days – no, I was banished from the theatre, again – to learn the lines, come back and play the character to his expectation or pack my bags and leave the course. He gave my role to another of my mates who had up to then been my double. For the next two days, I was paralyzed but finally, I saw the challenge and I took it. I was quite popular with my mates and many others in the department as was the mate who now had my role. The department was divided. Many of my mates would come to my room to help while others went to my double. It was a harrowing time. There was no technique that my helpers did not prescribe but finally, I got the lines! In eight days, I was ready!

My friend, the double, was also a budding reggae artiste at the time, with a growing popularity all over Port Harcourt. He had a string of shows and obviously did not have the time to work on the lines as I had. I was present when Ola Rotimi took him down. His was far longer than mine. I sympathized with him but that quickly changed to trepidation when he turned in my direction and ordered me to go on! He never asked if I was ready. He just barked, 'Yes?!' in my direction. I played, everything, lines, blocking, character, according to the book. Professor Ola Rotimi smiled. He regarded the class and asked, 'No be am?' There was the usual chorus of 'Na am!' from my fellow actors. It was my first commendation from this man that took nothing less than the best. I was elated. I grew in confidence.

## And I started to love the theatre

Then it was time for the national tour of the production. We played in Nsukka, Ibadan, Jos, Ife and Lagos. Each stop was a memorable one and a milestone in the development of my relationship with the Man. In Jos, I fell seriously ill and had to be admitted in the hospital. He was the only one in the ensemble who could play my role and he already had the costume amended to his size when I showed up, a few minutes from show opening. I had insisted in the hospital that I wanted to be discharged.

He took one look at me and said, no. But he also saw that I really wanted to play that night and he allowed me, patting me on the back as he handed me the wardrobe. Through the play, he stood at the door and had a few men standing by with thick blankets, the lights ready to black out if I collapsed on stage and the men to evacuate me from stage immediately. I felt loved and appreciated, especially coming from a man that seemed impossible to affect – it was an extraordinary moment for me. He was human after all.

In Ibadan, we clearly had an exceptional show, I in particular because when we got back to camp in Emmanuel College, he sent for me where he sat with his students, shook my hand – the first time – and said a simple, 'well done'. Then he asked what I would like to drink. I refused his offer shyly; I was not familiar with this version of him and did not want to have to refund the money if he discovered an infraction later but he was quick to remind me that he knew I was one of the regulars at the Staff Club kiosk – he saw everything without letting on – and I should feel free. He gave me the exact cost of the bottle of beer and insisted that I sat with him and his small group.

My golden handshake, my induction into his stringently selected group of favoured students, my redemption, confirmation as an actor. He took the 'good' with equanimity but his wish, time, grooming, is intended for the exceptional and never missed an opportunity to openly commend it. I entered that space with the great Ola Rotimi that night. From then on, all I wanted was to deliver the best always.

Ola Rotimi, how do I see him? I think to him, drama is not supposed to be performed. It should be deliberately plotted to 'just happen', organic, real, it should be experienced, felt, in the telling of the story, it should able to suck you in making you an unaware participant and the Thrust Stage at The Crab, Uniport, which he designed, allowed him to express all of that, an instant connection with the audience.

Ola Rotimi, in my view, was a geometrist, a directorial philosophy that was sensitive to geometric lines and distances and served him in his trademark ingenious crowd control abilities on stage. He practiced a theatre form that had to be evocative as you find in his *Hopes of the Living Dead*, his stories variegated in an admixture that challenges the norm even while conforming, his proletariat inclination manifest in pieces like his 'If: Tragedy of The Ruled', ruthlessly honest yet respectful of the culture of the world of his characters, his passion for his convictions and commitment to his African antecedents in spite of his widely travelled and liberal world view, obvious in all his pieces. He was a master of realism.

## Ola Rotimi is the theatre we all still aspire to

He was the disciplinarian yet concerned father, teacher, strong leader, innovative director, unmatched dramatist, superb organizer.

He finally revealed his thoughts of me in his valedictory speech to my class. I was probably the most difficult student for him in my set and he was certain that I would not only fail, I was not likely to amount to much in the arts. I can only hope whatever I have since become does commend his effort and memory. I hope when he looks down from wherever he is, he nods his sagely head in approval.

The Ola 'Ola Rotimi' Gladstone Rotimi I knew, taught me beyond drama, the discipline of the performer, the limitless capacity of the director, the never-ending curiosity to know more, respect for words. He offered himself as a mirror for every detail of production, helping you to see what you only feel. He was a generous knowledge conduit, immortal dramatist.

If I have indeed become anything, I am hopeful that it is a reflection of him and to his eternal credit.

# CHAPTER EIGHT

## Ola Rotimi: Ingenuity and Dexterity at Work

*Austin Awulonu*

When on the 18th of August 2000 the news broke, that Prof Ola Rotimi had transitioned to the great beyond, the grief was both personal and general. Generally, it was a colossal loss to the creative world, especially African theatre and, in particular, Nigerian Theatre. The loss was not just because he was a great and renowned playwright but even more so because Ola Rotimi was an *unputdownable* director who embodied everything good about the art of directing. He took Total Theatre to a whole new level in his productions. On a personal level, Ola Rotimi was a major influence of my directing craft.

I met him while I was studying for my degree at the Dramatic Arts Department of Obafemi Awolowo University in Ile Ife. It was absolute joy for us students when he showed up in the Department to direct *Hopes of the Living Dead* which was the Convocation Play for that year. Like most people of my generation, my first encounter with Ola Rotimi was before then though. It was through his play, *The Gods Are Not To Blame.* That play text was one of those in the Literature in English curriculum for secondary schools in the eighties. Having been dazzled by his comprehensively successful adaptation of Sophocles' *Oedipus Rex*, it was a massive privilege for me to finally meet the celebrated playwright in person. That meeting, that meeting …

I sighted Prof, as we were wont to call him, in the foyer of the Pit Theatre as I walked through the departmental gate and I was immediately star struck. Could that be him? Could that be the man? The legendary Prof Ola Rotimi who wrote *The Gods Are Not To Blame*? Could that really be him standing a few metres away from me? Could it be him? A thousand and one questions raced through my mind but there was no mistaking it! It was him! The face was exactly as it was in that monochrome picture on the back cover page of the book I read and re-read so many times that I had lost count. It was him. The glasses, the beard, everything was in place. Just as in that picture. It was him. Maybe some strands of grey now that were not present in the picture but it was him. It is him. O-la-Ro-ti-mi! In the flesh! Wow!

I went over to pay my homage and Rotimi, with arm extended went, "move back, you want to measure height with me?" He says this in a way only him could manage. It was neither a joke nor a rebuke. It was just a consternating statement. I was neither offended nor amused. Just consternated. What did I do wrong? Before I could fathom it, *voila*, he came to my rescue. To put this consternated young man at ease, he proceeded to ask about my studies, general welfare and all. Was that persona or anima? I was intrigued. There and then I knew, come what may, I must work with this man!

It is not for nothing that Prof Ola Rotimi was called master of the Crowd among several other sobriquets. This particular appellation speaks to his unrivalled dexterity at placing actors on the stage to telling effect. To however limit his directorial genius to mere blocking of the play will be a great disservice to a quintessential director who out-distanced his contemporaries in doing what he did best. To be in Ola Rotimi's theatre is to be enthralled by the entire one thousand and one appurtenances available to the director for fashioning his craft. He led from the front. Every director knows that once you don the director's hat you at once step into unparalleled leadership responsibilities. Your orchestra of men and materials await you for guidance because on this journey of creating the magic called theatre, you are their compass, coach, father, mother, psychologist, psychiatrist, teacher, confidante and disciplinarian should the need arise. You are the Solomon in the room. Leadership mettle never knew a sterner test nor ever will.

For the staging of his play, *Hopes of the Living Dead*, Ola Rotimi set the tone for us at dawn. No sooner had he gathered the potential team together than he spelt out the terms of engagement: for the next twenty-one days, if you choose to come on board, you give me your body and I seize your soul. For the duration of this production, suspend all excuses and permissions. You are not permitted to report late to rehearsals, you are not permitted to be absent, you are not permitted to be sick. You are not permitted to ask for permission. Suspend all sicknesses. You are either in or out. Which would it be? Make your decision now while you have the opportunity.

This was two days before he started casting. Everyone was at liberty to make their individual decision. What would it be? We are talking of the legendary Ola Rotimi! Who was going to opt out? Certainly not me. We die here! Who was not going to be part of the production? Long story short, on casting day everyone was present. As a matter of fact, there were more people as word had obviously gone round that Ola Rotimi was casting for a play. I guess we all basically forbade our village people from troubling us during the entire period of the production. Be that as it may, not only did he set the tone for the production at dawn, he equally led from the front, boots on the ground. Not once did he show up late for rehearsals. He kept the team ticking by his impeccable discipline and professionalism. When the captain upholds such high standards, who dares flout them? Whereas discipline was non-negotiable with him, Rotimi was a humane director who knew when to wield the stick and when to offer a warm blanket.

A case in point was the day Man-nobi-God turned up late for rehearsal. To begin with that was not his name; at least until the said day. Man-nobi-God was actually the Assistant Stage Manager for the production. On this faithful day the young man arrives after the day's business had commenced. Everyone was shocked and worried because he had been quite dutiful from the onset. What could have gone wrong? Nobody dared talk. Knowing the ground rules, he remains outside unable to enter despite the entrance being wide open! He bade his time till there was a short break. Then, in he comes and lays prostrate on the ground. With a shaking voice and close to tears, he narrated his ordeal. Area boys had caused mayhem in his part of town thereby making commute next to impossible from that axis as transporters refused to work for fear of their vehicles being damaged or destroyed. The silence in Pit Theatre was deafening. Holding back tears he continued, "As a matter-of-fact sir, I had to trek for the better part of the journey to come to rehearsal." Ola Rotimi just looked at him with a fixed gaze as he narrated his story. Unsettled, ASM swore God and the high heavens to underscore the truthfulness of his narrative. Ola Rotimi let him finish. We waited. ASM waited. Nobody said a word. What would Director do? Rotimi turned to the young man, smiled and said, "Man nobi God, get something to eat and come and join us." He then went on to confirm the young man's story as he had witnessed the mob himself on his way to the rehearsal. Needless to say, from that point on, ASM became known as Man-nobi-God till the end of the production and long after.

Clearly, Ola Rotimi was very good at man management as well as dealing with group dynamics. He would take time to explain the rationale for his blockings such that the actors found them comfortable. Before you knew it, movements became so natural, easy on the eye and seamless. Was it because he knew directing students were members of the team? Maybe, maybe not. Could it be the innate teacher in him? Either way though, beyond being in the team as just a member of cast, I was intentionally there with all my senses wide open knowing full well that one production with a master will always be worth its weight in gold when staked against a million words in print. Watching Rotimi work was a matchless masterclass.

Rotimi's cast for this particular production of *Hopes of the Living Dead* was drawn from members of the Ifeversity Acting Company, students of Dramatic Arts and students from outside the Dramatic Arts Department. It is to his credit that he managed the inherent idiosyncrasies and complexes in the group while sufficiently inspiring each and every one, particularly the students, to deliver stellar performances. His openness to what the actor brings to the table is immense. Charles O'Neill and myself doubled as Superintendent of Police playing on different nights. The interesting thing is that our interpretation was quite different yet Rotimi allowed both. Maximizing each player's natural attributes for the role was something he did dexterously well while not diminishing the character in any way. This was not peculiar to Charles and I because there were quite a number of roles that were double cast and the same was true for them in terms of actor play. His eye for details allowed him exploit the littlest manifestations that would serve the performance well for the ultimate good of the production.

He drilled the entire team to become a true ensemble. Be it dedicated rehearsals for players who needed to pick up or whole sections that was proving problematic, he had time allotted for it all. The Pressure Cooker Run was one he particularly used to whip everybody, cast and crew, into line through sharpened reflexes, focus, concentration and agility. The pressure Cooker Run also had a major psychological boost for actors as it settled them into knowing that they have the play canned. Rotimi's particularity with pictures is probably what earns him the sobriquet, master of the crowd. That can be misleading though because even when there were only two people on stage, he was particular about their positioning and the picture they cut. A more appropriate sobriquet would perhaps be master of pictures.

Doubtless the director must work with artistes from other departments of production to properly cook his pot of soup. Be it the set designer, wardrobe and props, light, sound etcetera, his ability to clearly convey his precise vision to these other artistes is a major component of how successful the production turns out. This is where I learnt from Prof the need for the director to be well prepared ahead of the job. He comes with consummate preparedness – a key asset for the director – to the table. He clearly lays his vision and thoughts on the table such that it becomes easy for others to latch onto it to drive their own imagination and muse. It became easy therefore for the actor to talk to Wardrobe because Wardrobe and Director are on the same exact page.

A master of moods, Rotimi, beyond the overall impact of the play, is clear on the effect he wants each scene to have on the audience. This is where his selection of songs and rendition style for each song shines through. I guess that comes with being such a wonderful singer himself because for this production, he was equally our choir master. He taught every song down to parts! For an exponent of the total theatre, I guess that is not really a surprise.

After such an encounter how does one distil all that has been imbibed? Ultimately, truth to tell is, one never really knows how much he has learned from such an experience or how much he has been influenced and impacted in the process in one fell swoop. So, *inter alia*, hindsight, the judge of all things, invariably, becomes the assessor of that. It is instructive though that during the course of my directing odyssey the question that has accosted me the most is in varying forms is, "Did you work with Ola Rotimi?" My humble answer has always been that I was privileged to. That privilege, apparently, greatly influenced my directing craft. It underscores the power of the man and his art to think that long after our paths crossed at the Pit Theatre of the Dramatic Arts Department in the picturesque campus of Obafemi Awolowo University, Ile Ife, I still get those questions.

# CHAPTER NINE

## Wole Soyinka on Ola Rotimi

### (An Interview)

*Bisi Adigun*

**BA**: So, Prof Wole Soyinka, thank you very much for taking out time to speak to me today.

**WS**: You are more than welcome

**BA**: Can you imagine that it's 20 years today that Professor Ola Rotimi left us?

**WS**: I must say it is very difficult. I have been to Ife a few times; both the university and the city. He opened up Ori Olokun centre, he was part of the team, Crowder and so on. But he, his company was really the dynamo behind that whole cultural centre with his performances and productions. And so each time I go there I remember him. And, of course, his son, Kole*, celebrated him; he invited me to lecture in his memory a number of years ago. So, somehow, I have always kept in touch with him. One more point or connection between us, when I was in exile was his encounter with some brutal soldiers on the road which he narrated to me personally. It is something which has stayed with me. I mentioned it in one of my books.

**BA**: Prof, I know you mentioned the personal story he told you in your 2006 autobiography, *You Must Set Forth At Dawn*, but could you please share this story with some of the people that have not yet read the book?

**WS**: Well, he met these brutes on the road, there used to be road blocks and so on. And then these soldiers of course took pleasure in humiliating the civilian population. And the more grammar they sensed that you spoke even before you opened your mouth, the greater the humiliation they wanted to give you. And

---

* During the course of publishing this book, Prof Wole Soyinka made time out of his busy schedule to locate the lecture that he gave in honour of Ola Rotimi at Duke University on September 17, 2004, from which he extracted the blurb included at the back cover of this volume.

sometimes when there were long queues and these soldiers were examining the vehicles, they would sometimes, they were more than one, they would sometimes pass a vehicle, especially if you were in a station wagon which is open on all sides, which was what Ola was driving.

One of the soldiers inspecting, took a look inside and waved him to go along. Well, poor Ola, he met another soldier who was examining other vehicles, stopped him, he said he had jumped the queue. The more Ola tried to explain to him that his own colleague had passed him, the more infuriated that soldier was. And Ola was with him family, his wife and his children, I think two of them and so told Ola to come out, and told him to turn his back and Ola said what? And he said: "Turn your back, I am going to whip you for jumping the queue. I was not there, I was not present, but that moment has lived with me in a tortured way because I have always asked myself: "What would I have done in the same circumstances?" When he told me, I thought: "What would have been my reaction?"

Anyways, Ola hesitated quite a while, then the man cocked his gun and was going to shoot him on the spot. And Ola said, "I looked at my wife and I looked at my child and I said am I going to turn her into a widow and my children into orphans?" So, he turned his back and this man lashed him several times. It would have been better if I had seen it, but it is worse I think imagining it and I am asking myself: "What would I have done in circumstances like that?"

**BA**: Prof, a lot of people will not know the kind of relationship that existed between you and Ola Rotimi. Please can you tell us a little bit about your relationship.

**WS**: At the beginning there was a kind of weariness. He got to Ife, I was in Ibadan, I was in exile for some time then I came to Ibadan, then to Ife and he was already firmly established and people like conflict, they thought there will be some rivalry, that kind of nonsense. So, I was just looking at all of them, listening to the comment. We took to each other immediately, and I used to attend his rehearsals. He was very deft with crowd scenes in his production. So, I used to go and spy on him, and we got on very well and he used to come to the house when I was in Ife, we had a marvelous relationship. It was that intimate, that when I arrived from exile, he couldn't wait to talk to me about that incident.

**BA**: I see. But was there any play of his that you would have loved to produce or directed?

**WS**: His most popular play of course, the one which launched him on the Nigerian scene was *Kurunmi*. It was a Nigerian reconstruction and I think that is where his real mastery lay: in historic reconstruction, presentation and so on. But he was very versatile also, I remembered he experimented on theatre at the absurd. There was another one whose title I can't recall now.

**BA**: *Holding Talks*?

**WS**: Yes, *Holding Talks*. So again that was a very witty one. He was very versatile and it was marvelous see him changing genre.

**BA**: A lot of people have compared your work with his, do you think it is necessary?

**WS**: No, I don't compare my work with other people's work. That is for people like you to do, but I can talk very freely and comfortably about other people's work;

**BA**: Thank you very much Prof. One more question: you said you had opportunity to see him at work, what kind of a director would you consider him to be?

**WS**: I think he was the kind of director he wanted to be, and remember he studied theatre in the States and you could see that he spotted the kind of direction which would actually bring out his talent as a playwright. So, he was very conscious from the very beginning; he had a sense of historic sweep when he looked at a stage. That was the feeling I got about the way he reacted. So, speculating what kind of director he would have been, he would have been exactly that. Whichever way he went.

**BA**: So, was there any time both of you wanted to collaborate, to work together, maybe you wanted to direct his play or he wanted to direct your play?

**WS**: Well… we just worked in tandem. Once or twice// after I wrote *Death and the Kings Horseman*, would have wanted us to collaborate on that kind of production, because he would have done all the hard labour, I would have just sat and watched but told him what kind of interpretation I wanted. I would have loved to collaborate on a play like that but we never did.

**BA**: Do you remember any of his production that will remain with you?

**WS**: Oh, I think for most people *Kurunmi.* It was so graphic, it was so visual and that kind of direction, that kind of play sticks to the minds I think more than the more cerebral or theatre of the absurd like *Holding Talks.* I think his *Kurunmi* is the one which will stay with us.

**BA**: Sir, when I sent you my email, you mentioned to me that, just a day before I sent you the email, you came across a manifesto written by Ola Rotimi.

**WS**: Well at the beginning I just took it and put it aside and said let me take another look some other time. At the beginning, he was not overtly political, he just was 99% theatre no matter what the theme was. For instance, his *Kurunmi* was not geared to make any contemporary statement, he just loved presenting history on stage and making it dramatic, interesting and if anybody wanted to extract any lesson from it, that was their business. In other words, he did not try to make an overt statement with his early productions. However, coming back into Nigeria after a number of years, seeing what was going on around him, watching the kind of military distortion of society and also of course the social anomalies, he became drawn into social commentary, political commentary and he was no longer satisfied even with presenting those on stage and it came out to my surprise with this statement. As I said, I remembered it immediately, I remembered what was inside but I haven't refreshed my mind with it lately.

**BA**: Thanks so much for your time, Prof. I don't know if there is any other question that you would like me to ask. But if there is none, I would like you to say a few words to our attendants and our participants. Thank you very much for your time, Prof.

**WS**: Well, it is a pity that this exercise did not start early enough. I think we might have succeeded in trying to bring together those who were witnesses to or participants in that Ori Olokun period and to see Akinbola and Femi Euba – those who were present at the time, to see if we could have re-staged in his memory as close as possible as his own interpretation and presentation, that classic *Kurunmi.* This is something which I would have loved to see and be part of if Covid 19 had not scattered things and disrupted people's timetable, projections and so on, even bringing people together of course. However, it was great having known and worked with Ola Rotimi and it is great having to remember him.

# AFTERWORD

On behalf of Ola Rotimi's family I thank you all for attending this webinar. You could be anywhere else doing something important but you chose to be here today on a Tuesday morning. Some of you logged in at 5 am and 6 am in the US to join us. Thank you for joining. Several people worked hard to make this event successful and we thank you too.

By "We" I am referring to Prof Ola Rotimi's family. Both his biological and those grafted in. Over the years, I have gotten to know many of his students at home and abroad as well as those he worked with. There's one common thing that everyone in the Ola Rotimi household and his students/staff would tell you. That is, he could read your character very quickly, identify your creative talent even before you knew about it yourself and bring it out of you. Sometimes the process was pleasant and sometimes not so pleasurable. Especially if you had the proclivity to laziness, excuses or taking shortcuts. Bringing out the best in young people and watching them evolve into their greatest potential was like a personal mission for him.

So, while the world gave him accolades and awards for plays and written works, we his family knew of his third mission and the delight he got in watching his people on TV, Radio, Hollywood, BBC and, of course, Nollywood. He is described as the "Father of Nollywood" because of the paternal relationship he had with his students and staff who became Nollywood directors, producers, and actors, even though he himself did not produce movies.

Not everyone of his grafted children became a professional actor, director or playwright. The fact is, it didn't matter what your talent was, if he sees "it" in you, he will pull "it" out of you. Public administration, Business or Engineering whatever "it" is he sees in you was coming out, and he expected you to excel at "it". He believed that everyone was sent to earth with a mission. You were given the talents and everything necessary to fulfill that mission.

Just as the mango seed has everything in it to become a mango tree to provide fruit for others to eat, shade from the scorching sun and provide a home for birds. All it needs is soil and water and it would grow to fulfill its mission on earth. The same applies to human beings, and his duty was to provide the necessary fertilizer to make you bloom into the best version of yourself, not a carbon copy of himself. As a result, he never insisted any of his children become playwrights, actors or directors like himself. Just as he did not become an engineer like his father or a public administrator like his grandfather, but was allowed to fulfill his mission with the talents that were deposited in himself at birth and strove to develop "it" to "its" fullest potential.

The same way he drove himself was the same way he drove those he loved. The personal discipline and result oriented training to be the best version of yourself and not a copy of someone else is evidenced in the lives of his children, students and anyone who worked with or for him. Including the house helps. Some of whom (House boys/house girls) became teachers, a famous sculptor, a flight engineer, university lecturer and a lawyer respectively. It didn't matter their tribe, religion, or economic background.

Notice I have not mentioned anyone's name. That's because there are so many of us that if I named everyone, we would be here for several hours and if I called just a few for brevity, those not called by name will take offense. "Why did you mention him and not me?" they would ask. We are building a website in his honour where the profiles of his people will be posted. We (biological children) are working with some of his adopted children to convert some of his plays into movies through the Ola Rotimi Foundation.

One question I often get is: Did any of the four children take up acting and writing? I will answer that question before you ask. Acting was as much a part of the Ola Rotimi household as eating. Everyone in the house went on stage except the dog. As a child you played the role of a child in his plays and acted all the way up through university when we graduated and moved on to our different careers in the Military, Education, Business Administration and Computer science. Biodun (Ola Junior) for example was a baby when he went on stage as Baby Odewale in the first performance of *The Gods Are Not To Blame* with Femi Robinson (He became the first Village headmaster on TV in the early 1970's) as King Odewale. In university, we spent so much time in the theatre that most people thought we were Theatre majors taking elective courses in Engineering, Political Science, Economics and Fine Arts; our real majors.

If the saying is, however, true that we get most of our genes from our grandparents, then Ola and Hazel Mae Rotimi's grandchildren are living proof of it. Amiah Mae Rotimi, their first granddaughter, has combined the Fine Artist talent of our mother (Hazel Mae Rotimi) and theatrical talents of Prof (Ola Rotimi) as a make-up artist for several music videos, and TV shows in the U.S. Kole Heywood Rotimi second grandchild has won several literary related awards between 2018 and 2020 prior to graduating from university just like his grandfather did as a Yale student. They include: the Mellon Mays Undergraduate Fellowship, Elizabeth Bruss Prize, James Charlton Knox prize, Pitch wars and the Francis-Chia Fellowship. It's too early to tell if the other grandchildren will take after one or both of their grandparents as they are still in high school and primary school.

Speaking on behalf of all his children and grands I thank you all once again for honouring our father on the twentieth anniversary of his passing and for keeping his name and works alive especially by implementing the life lessons you learnt from your contact with him either in person or through his literary works.

Thanks again and God bless.

Enitan J Rotimi
*18 August, 2020*

# NOTES ON CONTRIBUTORS

## Bisi Adigun

It was when Adigun saw the spectacular production of Ola Rotimi's *The Gods Are Not To Blame* as directed and narrated by the author himself, in 1976 at Ile-Ife that Adigun decided to become a theatre practitioner rather than a legal practitioner that his guardians would like him to be. Since then he has not looked back. Before joining Bowen University, Iwo, as a senior lecturer in October 2019, Adigun was an adjunct lecturer of African Theatre and Performance Studies at Trinity College, Dublin, Ireland, where he earned his PhD in Drama in 2013. In 2003, he founded Arambe Productions, Ireland's first and only African theatre company, for which, he produced and directed over 25 productions in Ireland, Nigeria and America. In 2007, the new version of JM Synge's *The Playboy of the Western World* which Adigun co-wrote with Irish writer Roddy Doyle had its world premiere at the famed Abbey Theatre in Ireland. In November 2023, the play had its American premiere production by Washington DC-based Solas Nua. Adigun's first volume of plays, *An Other Playboy, The Butcher Babes* and *Home, Sweet Home (Three Plays)*, was published by Universal Books UK in 2018. He is also the co-editor, with Duro Oni, of *The Soyinka Impulse: Essays on Wole Soyinka* (BookCraft, 2019). Adigun is currently co-editing with Duro Oni a book that will feature essay and interview contributions from over two dozens living Nigerian stage directors.

## Austin Awulonu

Born into the family of Eugene and Patricia Awulonu in Lagos in 1965, Austin trained at the Dramatic Arts Department of the Obafemi Awolowo University. His encounter with the inimitable Ola Rotimi and Chuck Mike as a directing student in that institution will leave telling marks on his art. Straight from the crucible of Great Ife his odyssey with the queen of the arts has continued to unravel; amassing variegated experiences across media at different junctures which further enriches his theatre expressions. In no particular order, Austin has directed *Three Sides to a Coin*; *Angst*; *Kuluso*; *Double Attack*; *The Gods Are Not To Blame*; *Childe Internationale*; *Out of The Deeps*; *Shelled Up*; *Red Card*; *The Divorce*; *The Marriage of Anansewa*; *Noah's Ark*; and several skits. For him, directing is essentially the harvesting and harnessing of the emotions to deliver a message to arouse a specific response from the audience. The emotions would include those of the actors and by extension those of the audience in combination with the emotion influencers of the theatre be they colour, sound, light, set, props or form.

## Bimbo Manuel

Bimbo Manuel is a Nigerian actor, writer and director. After studying Theatre Arts at the University of Port Harcourt, he proceeded to OGBC/OGTV in 1985 as a broadcaster. He later moved to NTA. His acting career commenced in 1986 while working at these organisations. His extensive body of work includes many stage, television and film credits, including some of the most iconic productions in the Nigerian entertainment industry. Some of these are *Saro, Wakaa, Checkmate, Fuji House of Commotion, Tinsel, Tango With Me, Dazzling Mirage, October 1, 93 Days, King of Boys,* to mention but a few. His writing credits include *Alhaji, Philomena, The Call* and *1960*. Manuel was nominated for Best actor in a supporting role at the 2013 Nollywood Movies Awards.

## Akanji Nasiru

Akanji Nasiru studied English and Theatre Arts at the University of Ibadan. For his PhD thesis, he wrote on "Communication and the Nigerian Drama in English", Ola Rotimi being one of the playwrights whose works examined. He was a foundation lecturer in Drama at Ahmadu Bello University, Zaria, and Performing Arts at the University of Ilorin. He had brief stints at Delta State University, Abraka, and Niger Delta University, Wilberforce Island, Bayelsa State. He retired from the University of Ilorin in 2013 and has been at Bowen University, Iwo, as a contract and visiting professor. In addition to teaching Theatre History and Dramatic Literature courses, he has written and directed many plays in and outside the university. He enjoys working with amateur drama groups in schools and churches. Among his published plays, *Our Survival* (Macmillan, 1985) won the maiden edition of the Competition of Third World Playwrights in 1981, and *The Rally* (Kraft Books, 2018) was runner-up in the 2018 edition of the NLNG Nigerian Prize for Literature. His interests include games, music and computer.

## Emmanuel Nwachuku

Dr Emmanuel Dike Eke Nwachuku has lectured for upwards of 23 years. Starting at The Lagos State University, in July 1998 and then University of Port Harcourt, from April 2011 (both in Nigeria) and he completed a two years and six months contract at Edna Manley College of the Visual and Performing Arts, Kingston, Jamaica, as the Head of Department, Technical theatre, and design in. August 2022. At press time of this publication, he was in the process of relocating, as Assistant Professor of Theatre design, to an undisclosed University. He holds a professional Certificate in Theatre Arts (CTA- Acting track- 1985) pioneer set, and a Bachelor of Arts degree in Theatre Arts (Directing track- 1990), both from the University of Port Harcourt, Nigeria. He also holds a master's degree in Performing Arts– Drama (Technical track-2006) – from the University of Ilorin, and a Doctorate degree in Theatre and Film studies - 2018, from the University of Port Harcourt, Nigeria. He has several academic publications in Journals and books to his credit, and has scripted, screen played, produced, directed and designed in many Nollywood (Nigeria) movies and also staged dramas.

## Olu Obafemi

Prof Olu Obafemi (FNAL, NMOM) is a retired Professor of English and Dramatic Literature of the University of Ilorin Nigeria where he taught for 44 years till his retirement in 2020. Professor Olu Obafemi is a playwright, novelist, poet, literary scholar, theatre director, translator and newspaper columnist. He was Chairman of the Board of the National Museums and Monuments, Director of Research, National Institute for Policy and Strategic Studies, and is currently the Pro- Chancellor and Chairman of the Governing Council, Federal University of Technology, Minna. Professor Olu Obafemi was President and Fellow of the Association of Nigerian Authors, Fellow and President of the Nigerian Academy of Letters (FNAL), Fellow and Trustee of the Society of the Nigerian Theatre Artists (fsonta), Fellow of the English Scholars Association of Nigeria (fesan) and a member of the Board of Trustees of the Nigerian Media Merit Award. Professor Olu Obafemi serves on many Committees of educational Agencies of the National Universities Commission, (NUC), Tertiary Education Fund (Tetfund) and JAMB. He is a Member of the NLNG Advisory Board of the Nigeria Prize for Literature. He was Chairman of the Take-off Committee of the Atiba University, Oyo, Oyo State. Professor Olu Obafemi is the Sole Recipient of the 2018 Nigerian National Order of Merit (NNOM).

## Duro Oni

Professor Duro Oni's research interests are in Theatre Arts Design and Aesthetics and the Nigerian Film Industry. He was Deputy Vice-Chancellor at the University of Lagos from 2013 to 2017, Dean Faculty of Arts from 2009 to 2013 and Head, Department of Creative Arts from 2006–2009. He was also the Chief Executive of the Federal Government Parastatal, Centre for Black and African Arts and Civilization from 2000-2006. Professor Duro Oni has ten books and over 60 articles in national and international outlets. He holds the BFA and MFA Degrees from the California Institute of the Arts and a Ph.D. in Theatre Arts from the University of Ibadan. Some of his recent publications include: *Striking Expressions: Theatre and Culture in National Development* (2017), *The Soyinka Impulse: Essays on Wole Soyinka* edited with Bisi Adigun (2019) and *Larger than His Frame II: Critical Studies and Reflections on Olu Obafemi* edited with Sunday Ododo (2021), The National Theatre and the Search for a Collective Identity of the Nigerian State (2022). He is currently the President of the Nigerian Academy of Letters.

## Julie Umukoro

Prof. Julie Umukoro hails from Ase in Ndokwa East Local Government Area of Delta State, Nigeria. She is a Professor of Semiotics and Performance Studies, University of Port Harcourt, Port Harcourt. Her works cut across the different genres of prose, drama, and poetry and appeal to the sensibilities of a variety of audiences. Her creative works include *Adams Family*, *Marriage Coup*, and *Three Tales Three Tribes*. She is a woman of many parts: a social activist, a philanthropist, a practiced administrator, and a leading voice in the campaign for the girl-child education. Her grassroots interventions through partnerships and networking have enormously boosted her capacity-building projects for youths and women in Rivers and Delta States (Nigeria). She has collaborated with affiliate NGO groups such as Mission Africa and Health Matters Incorporated for community health outreaches; and Purdue Peace Project (PPP), an initiative of the University of Purdue USA, resulting in the championing of similar peace-building initiatives in Rivers State. One of her notable intervention projects for the education of the indigent child is the Adorable Kidz Scholarship Intervention for orphans. This intervention is serviced yearly through affiliate orphanage homes. Prof Julie Umukoro is a Fulbright scholar and has chaperoned several organizations. Leading examples are as follows: President, United States Government Exchange Alumni Association (USGEAAN), Rivers State Chapter; President,

Fulbright Association of Nigeria, Rivers state chapter; President, Association of Ndokwa Professionals in Academia (ANPA); and Woman Leader of the Ndokwa nation, a role in which she has clearly distinguished herself. She is happily married to Professor Matthew M. Umukoro, a Professor of Media and Communication Studies, and are blessed with children and grandchildren.

# INDEX

www.ingramcontent.com/pod-product-compliance
Lightning Source LLC
LaVergne TN
LVHW041107150826
845673LV00007B/1958

* 9 7 8 9 7 8 7 9 4 2 5 8 1 *